Restoring
GROWTH
in
PUERTO
RICO

Restoring
GROWTH
in
PUERTO
RICO

Overview and Policy Options

SUSAN M. COLLINS
BARRY P. BOSWORTH
MIGUEL A. SOTO-CLASS
Editors

CENTER FOR THE NEW ECONOMY
San Juan, Puerto Rico

BROOKINGS INSTITUTION PRESS
Washington, D.C.

Library of Congress Cataloging-in-Publication data
Restoring growth in Puerto Rico : overview and policy options / Susan M. Collins,
Barry P. Bosworth, and Miguel A. Soto-Class, editors.
    p.   cm.
Includes bibliographical references and index.
ISBN-13: 978-0-8157-1550-4 (pbk. : alk. paper)
ISBN-10: 0-8157-1550-1
1. Puerto Rico—Economic policy. 2. Puerto Rico—Economic conditions—1952–
I. Collins, Susan Margaret II. Bosworth, Barry, 1942– III. Soto-Class, Miguel A.
IV. Title.
  HC154.5.R43 2006
  338.97295—dc22   2006011190

9 8 7 6 5 4 3 2 1

The paper used in this publication meets minimum requirements of the
American National Standard for Information Sciences—Permanence of Paper
for Printed Library Materials: ANSI Z39.48-1992.

Typeset in Adobe Garamond

Composition by Circle Graphics
Columbia, Maryland

Printed by Victor Graphics
Baltimore, Maryland

Contents

Foreword

This book is the culmination of a collaborative effort between the Brookings Institution and the Center for the New Economy (CNE). Building on CNE's initial vision to develop a growth strategy for Puerto Rico, the two institutions undertook a research project pairing researchers from the island and the mainland. The resulting papers incorporate empirical analyses and distill policy implications of particular relevance to Puerto Rico at the outset of the twenty-first century.

The Brookings Institution first became involved in the analysis of the Puerto Rican economy in 1930 with the publication of *Porto Rico and Its Problems*. That publication was followed by a period of remarkable economic progress that continued up to the 1970s. More recently, the rate of economic progress has slowed and there has been little or no further convergence of living standards in Puerto Rico with those on the mainland. In particular, rates of poverty are unacceptably high. At the seventy-fifth anniversary of the 1930 report, it is appropriate to undertake a critical re-evaluation of the island's economy and to seek means of re-invigorating growth.

The editors wish to thank a number of individuals for their extremely valuable contributions to this project, notably Ramón Cao for his work with

James Alm. We were particularly saddened that one of the coauthors, Luis Rivera-Batiz, suffered a stroke and passed away on April 14, 2006. He was an active and valuable participant in this project.

We are grateful to Deepak Lamba Nieves and Sergio M. Marxuach Colón of the Center for the New Economy, as well as Starynee Adams, Gabriel Chodorow-Reich, and Kristin Wilson of the Brookings Institution for their assistance in organizing the project and preparing the volume. Also at Brookings, Eric Haven verified the chapters. Katherine Kimball edited the manuscript, while Carlotta Riba assisted with proofreading, and Julia Petrakis prepared the index. At CNE, we would like to thank Carla Alonso, Ana Sofía Allende, Sofía Stolberg, and Michelle Sugden for their support and assistance.

The views expressed in this book are solely those of the authors and should not be ascribed to the organizations or persons acknowledged above (or on the acknowledgments page) or to the trustees, officers, or staff members of either the Center for the New Economy or the Brookings Institution.

STROBE TALBOTT   MIGUEL A. SOTO-CLASS
Brookings Institution   *Center for the New Economy*

Preface

Puerto Rico has been the subject of numerous studies throughout the past three hundred years. Since very early in its history, both foreign and local observers have recorded their interpretations of, and judgments about, the island. Marshal Alejandro O'Reilly, who arrived in San Juan in April 1765, was one of the earliest. He identified three key elements of the island's economy that continue to play a role to this day: the large informal economy, the fragility of public finances, and the dependence on foreign transfers.

In the nineteenth century two reports stand out. First is the extensive survey conducted by Colonel George Dawson Flinter in the early 1830s, which describes trends that still resonate today, such as the remarkable openness of the Puerto Rican economy to international trade and the incidence of large-scale tax evasion. The other significant report from this period is the *Report on the Island of Porto Rico* by Henry K. Carroll, published in 1899 just after the change of sovereignty. Carroll, President McKinley's special commissioner for Puerto Rico, identified poverty and education as two of the principal issues affecting Puerto Rican social development. Both continue to be areas of concern.

The twentieth century brought a stream of studies and reports on Puerto Rico's economy and society. Two of these reports are particularly noteworthy for their comprehensiveness and importance in guiding policy. The first is *Porto Rico and Its Problems*, published by the Brookings Institution in 1930. This study, prompted by various groups of Puerto Rican private citizens, was a thorough examination of the island's social and economic landscape. Its coverage included education, public debt, public health, agriculture, trade, and the state public works. It contained a long list of recommendations, many of which were eventually implemented by the Puerto Rican government. The authors identified two distinct problems affecting the island, one economic, the other political. The economic one was "how to raise the incomes and standards of living of her people to something approaching parity with those prevailing in continental United States." The political one was "how to establish mutually satisfactory public relations between the Island and the mainland." Today, both issues remain at the very core of the island's political economy.

The other important study from this period was Harvey Perloff's *Puerto Rico's Economic Future: A Study in Planned Development*, published by the University of Chicago Press in 1950. This study, conducted at the request of the University of Puerto Rico, is a sobering assessment of the economic development of the island at mid century. It signaled the potential of export-led growth for Puerto Rico that came to be known as the "industrialization by invitation" program. Its recommendations, which dominated economic policy in Puerto Rico during the second half of the twentieth century, focused on attracting foreign capital, matching it with the excess pool of local labor, and exporting the resulting products to the rest of the world. By most accounts this model was relatively successful in jump-starting the Puerto Rican economy.

However, the Puerto Rican economy began to falter in the 1970s, as evidenced by the Tobin Report of 1975 and the Krepps Report of 1979. At the close of 2005, its performance presented an economic conundrum. From some perspectives, it has been quite successful. Living standards exceed those in the rest of Latin America, and some quality of life measures are comparable to those in the most highly developed countries. At the same time, after fifty years of intense social change and economic growth, close to half of the Puerto Rican population still lives under the U.S. poverty line, and this number shows no sign of declining.

By most criteria, Puerto Rico has created the conditions for strong sustained growth. It has increased educational attainment to OECD levels and made extensive investments in physical capital and infrastructure. In addition, Puerto Rico is one of the world's most open economies; and it has a strong institutional framework, built around protection of property rights and respect for the rule of law. By these standards, Puerto Rico should be growing much more rapidly. Why did growth slow down?

This question is the principal subject of the project that resulted in this book. Both Brookings and the Center for the New Economy (CNE) have strived to produce a balanced and fair assessment of the Puerto Rican economy, based on empirical data and independent analysis. In addition to critically examining the record of economic growth, this study also seeks to provide policy recommendations that can and should be implemented by the Puerto Rican and U.S. governments.

DEEPAK LAMBA NIEVES
SERGIO M. MARXUACH COLÓN
MIGUEL A. SOTO CLASS

Center for the New Economy
San Juan, Puerto Rico
April 2006

Acknowledgments

This project was entirely financed by the contributions of private citizens and enterprises in Puerto Rico. We are grateful to the following contributors who have provided financial support to this endeavor and encouraged an atmosphere of complete academic freedom for the project:

Churchill G. Carey, Jr.	Jaime Martí
Ángel Collado-Schwarz	Enrique Vila del Corral
José Enrique Fernández	Joaquín Viso
Antonio Luis Ferré	Triple S, Inc.

1

Introduction

SUSAN M. COLLINS, BARRY P. BOSWORTH,
AND MIGUEL A. SOTO-CLASS

At the close of the millennium, Puerto Rico was a tale of two economies. On the one hand, it had achieved some impressive economic
milestones. Per capita income was substantially higher than in the rest of
Latin America. On quality-of-life measures such as literacy rates, years of
schooling, and life expectancy it ranked close to the most highly developed
countries. But in other key dimensions, Puerto Rico appeared stuck under
an economic glass ceiling. Although they have been American citizens since
1917, nearly half of Puerto Rico's residents still lived below the U.S. poverty
line, and the income gap relative to the mainland was widening.

As a territory of the United States, Puerto Rico shares key U.S. institutions. In particular, the region operates under U.S. judicial, monetary, and
tariff systems. It is one of the world's most open economies, with free mobil-
ity of goods, services, capital, and labor to the large and prosperous U.S. market. One might expect these conditions to pave the way for rapid economic
development in Puerto Rico, with living standards converging steadily with
those enjoyed in the rest of the nation.

Indeed, in the decades following World War II, Puerto Rico was hailed as
a success story, sustaining impressive rates of economic growth and significantly raising domestic living standards. Its gross domestic product (GDP)

per worker rose from 30 percent of the U.S. average in 1950 to 75 percent in 1980, a remarkable achievement.

Since the early 1980s the economic situation on the island[1] has deteriorated. GDP growth has slowed substantially, and no further progress has been made in narrowing the gap with the U.S. mainland. Gross national income (GNI) per capita, a more appropriate measure of living standards, yields an even less favorable picture. While income per capita doubled from just over 20 percent of the U.S. average in 1950 to roughly 40 percent in the early 1970s, it has drifted back down to only about 30 percent more recently. Living standards in Puerto Rico are further from the U.S. average today than in 1970, and per capita income is only about half that of the poorest state.

Why did Puerto Rico's economic progress stall? And more important, what can be done to restore growth? These are the questions that motivated the Center for the New Economy and the Brookings Institution to undertake this collaborative research project. The objective was to examine Puerto Rico's economy and propose strategies for sustainable growth. Although it necessarily touches on political issues at times, no assessment of the alternative political options for the region was intended. Indeed, our economic analyses and proposed growth strategy are status neutral and will be relevant regardless of political regime.

The issues raised by Puerto Rico's puzzling economic performance are both important and interesting. Many Americans are unaware that the incomes of a large group of fellow citizens have remained far below the national average. More broadly, it is critical to understand why an economy with so many of the characteristics economists deem key to growth does not perform better. And as economic integration expands and deepens in Europe and elsewhere, it is more and more essential to understand which policy levers remain available for a small but very open peripheral economy to ensure that it does not fall behind.

A preliminary analysis of Puerto Rico's economic situation highlighted a set of overlapping concerns that appeared to be at the heart of Puerto Rico's economic difficulties. These included dimensions of labor supply and demand, entrepreneurship, the fiscal situation, financial markets, and trade. Puerto Rican and mainland experts were paired to study each of these topics, so as to ensure that the analysis was grounded in the relevant historical

1. We sometimes follow common parlance in using the phrases "on the island" and "on the mainland" to distinguish developments in Puerto Rico from those in the rest of the United States. In addition to the principal island of Puerto Rico, the Commonwealth of Puerto Rico also includes Vieques, Culebra, Culebrita, Palomino (known by some as the Spanish Virgin Islands), Mona, Monito, and various other isolated islands.

context. The authors met for an initial conference in San Juan in May 2004. Drafts of all their papers, as well as commentary by invited discussants, were presented at a second, academic-style conference in March 2005, also in San Juan. Complete versions of the revised analyses, as well as the discussants' remarks, are published in *The Economy of Puerto Rico: Restoring Growth,* the companion volume to this monograph.[2] This monograph summarizes each of the eight substantive papers in that volume. The final chapter, reproduced in its entirety, pulls together the lessons from these analyses and sets out a growth strategy for Puerto Rico.

In the next chapter, Barry P. Bosworth and Susan M. Collins examine the level and growth of production and income in Puerto Rico, setting the stage for the remaining chapters. Pulling together data from a variety of sources, they analyze why economic performance faltered, identify the main characteristics of the current economy, and highlight the key challenges for restoring sustained growth.

Per capita income in Puerto Rico is less than one-third that on the U.S. mainland. A substantial portion of this gap can be traced to Puerto Rico's strikingly low employment rate—and ultimately to its persistently low rates of labor force participation. Two chapters in the volume are devoted to examining the causes of this shortfall. Gary Burtless and Orlando Sotomayor carefully document implications of the generosity and structure of government transfer benefits available to Puerto Rico residents. María E. Enchautegui and Richard B. Freeman explore dimensions of what they term the "rich uncle (Sam) hypothesis"—that Puerto Rico's unique relationship with the United States has produced an economic environment that discourages work on both the supply and demand sides of the market. These studies reach similar policy conclusions: for example, that transfer programs should be redesigned in order to encourage work.

Puerto Rico has a remarkable record of educational development over the past forty years. However, as Helen F. Ladd and Francisco L. Rivera-Batiz document in chapter 5, concerns have emerged about deteriorating educational quality and growing inequities. They address the significant improvements in schooling that are now necessary if the commonwealth is to continue to use education as an engine of economic development.

Chapter 6 turns to the demand side of Puerto Rico's employment shortfall. Steven J. Davis and Luis A. Rivera-Batiz document the relatively underdeveloped state of the Commonwealth's private sector, examine some of its key implications, and propose actions that might be undertaken to

2. Collins, Bosworth, and Soto-Class (2006).

invigorate it. Of particular note, they show that the employment shortfall is concentrated in the private sector and that Puerto Rico's industry structure is grossly misaligned with the human capital mix of its population.

Puerto Rico's growing public debt and large recent budget deficits are particularly worrisome. James Alm critically assesses Puerto Rico's fiscal situation in chapter 7. While he addresses some features of public expenditure, his focus is the tax side, emphasizing a weak tax administration and the overuse of tax incentives, which he argues undermine the government's efforts to promote development.

While Puerto Rico cannot conduct an independent monetary policy, a long literature emphasizes the importance of finance for economic development. In the eighth chapter, Rita Maldonado-Bear and Ingo Walter present detailed summaries of each component of the commonwealth's financial sector, including the Government Development Bank, and suggest approaches for enhancement.

Furthermore, Puerto Rico has a small but extremely open economy. Thus, although trade is a central determinant of its economic performance, it cannot conduct an independent trade policy. In chapter 9, Robert Z. Lawrence and Juan Lara examine Puerto Rico's trade experience and implications for external adjustment, employment, and growth. Their recommendations concentrate on industrial policy and the strengths and weaknesses of alternative approaches.

In the final chapter, Bosworth and Collins present a set of policy recommendations for restoring growth in Puerto Rico. Drawing on the analysis and conclusions of the preceding chapters, they focus on increasing employment, improving the quality of education, upgrading infrastructure, and fixing government finances.

2

Economic Growth

BARRY P. BOSWORTH AND SUSAN M. COLLINS

In their chapter, Barry Bosworth and Susan Collins conduct an extensive analysis of Puerto Rico's growth performance and its determinants. The island enjoyed very rapid economic growth in the decades immediately after World War II, comparable to that achieved by the so-called Asian Tigers.[1] Over the past twenty-five years (since the early 1980s), however, growth in income per capita slowed substantially, and progress in narrowing the income gap with the mainland has stalled.

Figure 2-1 highlights two critical aspects of Puerto Rico's growth performance. The top line shows output per worker in Puerto Rico, as a proportion of the corresponding measure for the United States. Gross domestic product (GDP) per worker, a measure of the productivity of Puerto Rican workers, rose from just 30 percent of the U.S. average in 1950 to 75 percent in 1980, a remarkable achievement. However, it is also clear that growth slowed in subsequent years and that Puerto Rico has made little further progress in catching up with the mainland.[2] The second line in figure 2-1 shows gross national income (GNI) per capita, or the total income accruing

---

1. Baumol and Wolff (1996).
2. Numerous prior studies helped inform this analysis. Among the most helpful were: Dietz (2002 and 2003), Estudios Técnicos (2003), Padin (2003), Pantojas-Garcia (1999), Rivera-Batiz and Santiago (1996), and United Nations (2004).

Figure 2-1. *GDP and GNI, Puerto Rico Relative to the United States, 1950–2004*
Index (United States = 1.0)

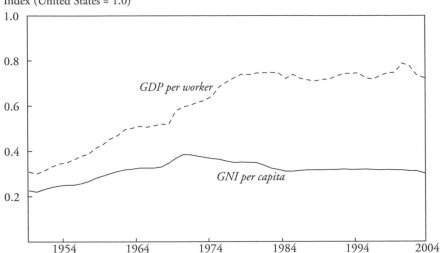

Source: Data from Puerto Rico Planning Board; authors' calculations, as explained in text.

to residents of the island, which is a more accurate measure of the average income of Puerto Ricans. This yields a dramatically different and much less favorable picture of the island's economic performance. Income per capita rose from a little over 20 percent of the U.S. average in 1950 to roughly 40 percent by the early 1970s. But it has drifted back down to only about 30 percent in recent years.

The gap in per capita incomes can also be related to underlying differences in the proportion of income that accrues to residents, productivity, labor utilization, and the age structure of the population. This is shown by the following equation:

$$GNI\big/capita = \left(GNI\big/GDP\right) \times \left(GDP\big/E\right) \times \left(E\big/P_{lf}\right) \times \left(P_{lf}\big/P\right),$$

where

$GNI\big/GDP$ = the proportion of income from production that accrues to residents,

$GDP\big/E$ = production per worker,

$E\big/P_{lf}$ = the proportion of the population aged sixteen and over that is employed, and

$P_{lf}\big/P$ = the proportion of the population that is aged sixteen and over (demographics).

This decomposition yields four crucial insights. First, as already noted, Puerto Rico made extraordinary progress in closing the productivity gap with the mainland, with productivity per worker rising from roughly 30 percent in 1950 to 75 percent by 1980. However, it has achieved no further progress in the twenty-five years since then. Second, Puerto Rico experienced a significant demographic change relative to the United States. In 1950, Puerto Rico's population was very young, with only half its residents aged sixteen and over. Today the share of the population of working age has reached 76 percent, equal to that on the mainland.

The third point concerns labor force participation. Between 1950 and 1980 the employment rate declined by a fourth (from 49 to 36 percent)—at a time when it was rising in the United States. Although the situation has improved somewhat since 1980, Puerto Rico's employment rate is still only about two-thirds of that in the United States and is also far below that of any OECD country, including Mexico. Thus the favorable effects of demographic change for the growth in income per capita have been wiped out by a surprising and large decline in the proportion of the labor-force-aged population that is employed.

Finally, a very large proportion of the income earned within Puerto Rico is now transferred abroad. In 1950, Puerto Rico had a net surplus of factor income transactions with the rest of the world, largely because of the wages of Puerto Ricans working for the U.S. government. However, in subsequent years the net wage payment surplus has been overwhelmed by outflows of capital income paid on foreign direct investments in Puerto Rico. Net capital outflow grew from 2 percent of GDP in 1950 to 15 percent in 1975, and then skyrocketed to 36 percent of GDP by 2004. Thus, GNI had fallen to just 62 percent of GDP by 2004, from 107 percent in 1950.[3]

The 936 Provisions

The U.S. tax code has had a major impact on Puerto Rican economic activity as well as on the measurement of this activity, including the evolution of net capital flows discussed above. Most notably, section 936 of the Tax Reform Act of 1976 added a tax credit on income earned in Puerto Rico and repatriated by U.S. firms. The exemption expired in 2005, but for thirty years it provided a strong incentive for U.S. firms to overstate profits earned in Puerto Rico. For example, mainland firms normally report a low value for raw materials shipped to Puerto Rico and a high value for final products

3. Puerto Rico Planning Board, U.S. Bureau of Economic Analysis, and authors' calculations.

exported from the island. The difference between the two is the measure of their contribution to value added in Puerto Rico. However, the difference also includes the contribution of research and development that was conducted on the mainland. In effect, companies can report such expenses in the United States (where the tax rate is high) while recording the returns in Puerto Rico (where the tax rate is zero).

Available data strongly support this hypothesis. Among drug firms, which in 1997 accounted for 57 percent of all 936 credits, net return on stockholders' equity equaled 112 percent for firms in Puerto Rico, compared with 25 percent for the U.S. industry as a whole. In the broader category of chemicals, the ratio of capital income to employee compensation averaged 10.5 in Puerto Rico over the period 1987–2001, and 2.1 in the United States.[4] Differences in relative factor returns of this magnitude cannot credibly be attributed to differences in the underlying production processes.

Income shifting by 936 corporations has greatly distorted measurement of output and productivity growth in manufacturing. According to official statistics, labor's share of value added in manufacturing fell from an average of 50 percent of gross product in the period 1950–70 to 14 percent by 2004. The distortion has grown over time as the chemical industry, which accounts for the bulk of 936 activity, increased in size from 11 percent of manufacturing net income in 1970 to over 60 percent in 2004. Bosworth and Collins therefore develop two "adjusted" measures of gross product in manufacturing.

The first, and more extreme, assumes that labor's share of total manufacturing gross product remains constant after 1970 at its 1969–70 average of 50 percent. Thus the entire rise in capital's share since 1970 is attributed to income shifting by 936 corporations. The second alternative limits the adjustment to a constant labor share (23 percent) within the chemical industry. This alternative recognizes that chemicals production is highly capital intensive (reflected in its relatively low labor share). However, it assumes no increase in the degree of capital intensity after 1970. It also allows the chemicals industry to grow as a share of total manufacturing.

The result is a dramatic downward adjustment of manufacturing output over the period 1970 to 2004. Relative to official data for 2004, the first measure cuts the estimates of manufacturing output and economy-wide GDP by 72 percent and 31 percent respectively. Using the second measure,

4. Based on data from Contos and Legel (2000, tables 1, 12), and Puerto Rico Planning Board (2003b, tables 10, 13).

which limits the adjustment to the chemical industry, 2004 manufacturing output and economy-wide GDP are reduced by 45 percent and 17 percent respectively. This represents a 1.7 percent reduction in the annual growth of manufacturing and a 0.7 percent reduction in the annual growth of aggregate output and productivity.

More broadly, the authors find a number of shortcomings in the measurement of real economic activity in Puerto Rico. The basic structure of the consumer price index (CPI) has changed very little since 1954 and is considered outdated. In recent years, the CPI has reported a rate of inflation nearly three times that of the consumer price deflator based on the expenditure accounts. Prices in individual categories such as food and apparel also show substantial divergence from the mainland. These differences suggest Puerto Rico could improve the quality of economic analysis by updating its statistical framework.

Growth Accounting

Bosworth and Collins use a growth accounting framework to decompose increases in output per worker into the separate contributions of changes in physical capital per worker, education, and a residual estimate of total factor productivity (TFP). The procedure assumes competitive factor markets and a uniform return to education, and allows the authors to examine the proximate causes of growth.[5] Table 2-1 summarizes the resulting growth accounts for the total economy over the entire period as well as individual subperiods. The top panel presents the analysis based on the published measure of GDP while the second panel uses the alternative measure that adjusts for income shifting within the chemicals sector. As shown in column 1, real GDP grew at an average rate of 4.9 percent per year over the full period and peaked at a growth rate near 8 percent in the 1960s. However, growth slowed substantially in later decades. The pattern of growth in output per worker is very similar to that for output alone, although the 1980s stand out as a particularly bad decade. In columns 4–6, growth in output per worker is partitioned among the contributions of physical capital per worker, education (human capital), and the TFP residual.

The analysis suggests that Puerto Rico's growth experience can be divided into two broad periods. First, during the period 1950–75, labor productivity increased rapidly, averaging a remarkable 5 percent annually. Improvements in physical capital per worker accounted for roughly half of

5. Bosworth and Collins (2003).

Table 2-1. *Sources of Growth, Puerto Rico, Selected Years, 1950–2004*
Percent

Period	Output (per year)	Employment (per year)	Output per worker (per year)	Contribution by component		
				Physical capital per worker	Human capital	Total factor productivity
Official output						
1950–2004	4.9	1.4	3.4	1.5	0.6	1.3
1950–60	5.4	−0.6	6.1	3.0	0.6	2.3
1960–70	7.9	2.3	5.5	2.5	0.8	2.2
1970–80	4.3	1.0	3.3	1.4	0.8	1.1
1980–90	3.6	2.5	1.1	−0.4	0.5	1.0
1990–2004	3.7	1.7	2.0	1.1	0.4	0.5
1950–75	6.0	0.7	5.2	2.7	0.7	1.7
1975–2004	3.9	1.9	2.0	0.4	0.5	1.0
Adjusted output, version 2 [a]						
1950–2004	4.5	1.4	3.0	1.5	0.6	0.9
1950–60	5.4	−0.6	6.1	3.0	0.6	2.3
1960–70	7.9	2.3	5.5	2.5	0.8	2.2
1970–80	3.7	1.0	2.7	1.4	0.8	0.5
1980–90	3.0	2.5	0.5	−0.4	0.5	0.4
1990–2004	2.9	1.7	1.3	1.1	0.4	−0.2
1950–75	5.9	0.7	5.1	2.7	0.7	1.6
1975–2004	3.2	1.9	1.3	0.4	0.5	0.4

Source: Authors' calculations as described in text and Bosworth and Collins (2006), appendix 2C.
a. Adjusted at the level of the chemicals industry.

this improvement. Improvements in the educational attainment of the workforce added another 0.7 percent a year. The remainder, 1.7 percent a year, can be traced to improvements in TFP.

However, productivity growth slowed sharply after the mid-1970s, weakening dramatically in the 1980s, and improving only modestly in the 1990s. What happened? Much of the story is in the failure of capital accumulation to maintain the prior rate of capital deepening (increasing capital per worker). From 1950 to 1975, Puerto Rico resembled the East Asian economies, with capital per worker catching up with the mainland. After 1975 the slowing of capital deepening, from 2.7 to 0.4 percent a year, accounts for two-thirds of the falloff in labor productivity growth. There have also been slowdowns in the contributions of human capital and TFP, but these decelerations were much less dramatic. In contrast, employment growth actually accelerated after 1975, offsetting part of the impact of the productivity growth slowdown on GDP growth.

The weakness of capital accumulation is especially evident in the late 1970s and 1980s. The total investment rate plunged from 28 percent of GDP in 1972 to 15.5 percent in 1977, and then drifted down to a low of 9.5 percent in 1983. Although there was a small falloff in public construction, and a significant drop in housing, most of the decline was in private business investment. Despite some recovery in the private component after 1985, investment has never returned to the rates achieved in the 1960s. At 15 percent of GDP, the current rate is only sufficient to support a long-term GDP growth of about 2.5 percent per year.[6]

The lower panel of table 2-1 shows how these results are affected by adjusting GDP to reflect activities of 936 corporations. Version 2, which indexed nominal output in the chemicals industry to the growth in labor compensation, reduces the annual growth of overall GDP per worker during the period 1975–2004 from 2 to 1.3 percent. Since the adjustment does not alter the contributions of physical or human capital, all of the change contributes to lowering the residual growth in TFP. The result is a growth in TFP of just 0.4 percent per year, compared with 1.0 percent using the official data. The deterioration in growth performance from the 1970s to the 1980s is particularly marked in the 1980s, with the increase in labor productivity slowing from 2.7 to 0.5 percent. Labor productivity growth picks up a bit after 1990 owing to a larger contribution of capital deepening, but the change in TFP turns negative. The adjustment greatly strengthens the pattern of steadily deteriorating productivity performance after 1975 that was already evident in the official data. It also suggests that the problem extends beyond a weakening of capital formation to include a large deceleration of the growth in TFP.

Sector Productivity

The authors also examine productivity changes at the sectoral level. They find that the shift out of agriculture over the past half century has been dramatic. In 1954 agriculture accounted for a third of total employment and 17 percent of output. By 1977 it represented only 6 percent of employment

---

6. The computation is based on the assumption that the capital stock, currently twice that of GDP, would need to grow at the same rate of output. The capital stock is constructed with a 5 percent rate of annual depreciation. Thus a gross rate of investment of 15 percent translates into a net investment rate of 5 percent of GDP, or 2.5 percent of the capital stock.

and 3 percent of output. Today its share of output has fallen to less than 1 percent. Because worker productivity was much greater in the goods- and services-producing sectors, the large shift of employment out of agriculture added about 0.8 percent to the annual growth of labor productivity in the period 1954–77. However, the much smaller employment shift after 1977 has only added 0.4 percent to annual growth since then.

Adjusting output for the overstatement of income in the chemicals industry reduces the goods-producing share of output in 2004 from 49 percent to 35 percent. The adjusted data suggest a growing role for both goods and services production. In contrast, employment data suggest a declining role for both agriculture and goods production, with an increasingly dominant role for services production. Last, while the post-1975 slowdown in productivity growth is evident in all three sectors, it is particularly pronounced in goods-producing industries.

International Comparisons

Table 2-2 provides some context for Puerto Rico's growth experience by contrasting it with experiences elsewhere. It is clear that Puerto Rico did achieve considerable convergence with the United States, given growth in output per worker well above that of the mainland. However, it is also clear that nearly all of that convergence occurred before 1980. The adjusted output version suggests that Puerto Rico actually lost ground after 1980. Furthermore, Puerto Rico's catch-up can be traced primarily to a more rapid rate of physical capital accumulation and to substantial progress in narrowing the educational attainment gap. The commonwealth has performed less well in catching up to the mainland level of TFP.

Table 2-2 also shows that Puerto Rico has performed well relative to an average of eighty-four countries that constitute about 95 percent of world GDP. The most distinguishing feature is an unusually large contribution of improvements in educational attainment. Puerto Rico's growth performance looks particularly favorable in comparison with growth in Latin America. This is primarily because Puerto Rico avoided the financial (exchange rate) crises that periodically disrupted growth elsewhere in the region. Thus official measures of its TFP growth stay positive after 1980, despite the general growth slowdown. On the other hand, the adjusted output measure reveals that average growth in output per worker falls short after 1980. Since then, Puerto Rico was unable to keep up with the newly industrializing economies of East Asia, which achieved nearly as strong gains in educational attainment but also maintained rapid physical capital accumulation.

Table 2-2. *Sources of Growth, Selected Regions, Selected Years, 1960–2000*
Percent

Country or region	Output	Output per worker	Physical capital per worker	Education	Factor productivity
Puerto Rico (published)					
1960–2000	5.0	3.1	1.1	0.6	1.3
1960–80	6.3	4.2	1.9	0.8	1.5
1980–2000	3.9	2.0	0.4	0.4	1.2
Puerto Rico (adjusted)					
1960–2000	4.5	2.6	1.1	0.6	1.2
1960–80	5.8	3.8	1.9	0.8	1.0
1980–2000	3.2	1.4	0.4	0.4	1.3
United States					
1960–2000	3.4	1.6	0.4	0.3	0.9
1960–80	3.6	1.5	0.1	0.6	0.8
1980–2000	3.3	1.8	0.6	0.1	1.1
World[a]					
1960–2000	4.0	2.3	1.0	0.3	0.9
1960–80	4.6	2.7	1.2	0.4	1.1
1980–2000	3.5	1.9	0.8	0.3	0.8
Latin America[b]					
1960–2000	4.0	1.1	0.6	0.4	0.2
1960–80	5.9	2.8	1.0	0.3	1.4
1980–2000	2.3	−0.4	0.1	0.4	−0.9
East Asia[c]					
1960–2000	6.7	3.9	2.3	0.5	1.0
1960–80	7.3	4.1	2.3	0.5	1.2
1980–2000	6.6	3.9	2.4	0.5	0.9
Mexico					
1960–2000	4.7	1.3	0.6	0.5	0.2
1960–80	6.9	3.1	1.1	0.4	1.6
1980–2000	2.7	−0.4	0.2	0.5	−1.1
Ireland					
1960–2000	4.9	4.0	1.3	0.3	2.3
1960–80	4.6	3.9	1.7	0.3	1.8
1980–2000	5.5	4.1	0.9	0.3	2.9

Source: Data from Bosworth and Collins (2003) and as described in Bosworth and Collins (2006), appendix 2C; authors'calculations.
a. Eighty-four countries.
b. Twenty-three countries.
c. Excluding China; seven countries.

Puerto Rico's growth is often compared to that in Mexico and Ireland. Mexico is of interest as a nearby Latin American country, sometimes seen as a competitor in view of its expanding economic ties to the United States and its considerably lower labor costs. Despite some recovery in recent years, Mexico still suffers in comparison, both because of its disastrous 1980s economic experience and because of its 1994–95 financial crisis. Ireland is a small island economy of nearly identical population that has performed extraordinarily well in the decade since the mid-1990s. Ireland's growth has resulted mainly from strong improvements in employment and TFP, in contrast to the emphasis on capital accumulation in East Asia. That focus has been particularly evident since 1990. As a highly successful island economy that overcame a prior period of slow growth, Ireland may offer some guidance for Puerto Rico.

Labor Inputs

This analysis highlights two features of the Puerto Rican labor force that have had strong impacts on the island's growth performance. First, relatively few Puerto Ricans are employed. Second, the quality of the workforce has increased substantially over time. Separate chapters are devoted to each of these subjects; thus they are discussed only briefly here.

Puerto Rico's employment rate is only two-thirds of the comparable rate on the mainland. This implies that raising the Puerto Rican rate to the mainland level (with unchanged income per worker) would increase total island income by 50 percent. Much of the difference in employment rates between Puerto Rico and the mainland stems from a lower labor force participation rate. The labor force participation rate declined for both men and women between 1950 and 1980, and has since remained at around 80 percent and 60 percent of the mainland level, respectively. High social transfers not tied to work incentives emerge as the most likely explanation for the low participation rates. The phase-in of the U.S. minimum wage in the late 1970s and migration to the mainland may also have helped to drive down participation rates.[7]

In addition to its low labor force participation, Puerto Rico has also long had a very high rate of unemployment. In the early years, this accounted for much of the difference in the employment-to-population ratio between the United States and Puerto Rico. The reasons for such a persistently high rate remain unclear. However, some observers argue that the minimum wage

7. Castillo-Freeman and Freeman (1992).

may have had a major effect—emphasizing that the minimum has been so much higher relative to the average wage in Puerto Rico than in the United States.

Puerto Rico has made remarkable gains in improving the educational skills of its workforce. The international comparisons presented here show that only South Korea reported as large a gain from increased educational attainment. Indeed, from 1950 to 2000 average years of schooling went from five to twelve. Among employed persons aged twenty-five to thirty-four, any difference with the mainland has vanished, as Puerto Ricans' average attainment equaled 14.4 years, compared with 14.5 years on the mainland. While concerns about educational quality caution against associating increased attainment directly with improvements in the quality of the workforce, the dramatic size of the gains realized and the implied micro-returns to education derived from wage data suggest that the increases in educational attainment have contributed substantially to growth.

Still, wage rates on the island have failed to converge toward mainland levels over the past twenty-five years. This lack of convergence at the aggregate level contrasts with the finding of increased educational attainment and positive returns to education, but conforms with the notion that labor productivity growth has slowed. Puerto Rico's average wage (54 percent of the mainland average) is in line with the adjusted estimate of Puerto Rican labor productivity (58 percent of the mainland level).

A final point on the contribution of labor to economic growth concerns the underground economy. The presence of a large informal economy would provide one explanation for the low labor force participation rate, as individuals working in underground activities may not report their work effort. A growing informal economy would also distort the accuracy of output statistics. Bosworth and Collins analyze previous surveys of the underground economy in Puerto Rico, discrepancies among tax, employment, and output statistics, and conduct an analysis using growth in electricity demand to estimate the size of the Puerto Rican informal sector. Although each method has weaknesses, taken together they suggest that Puerto Rico has a vibrant informal sector. However, none of the evidence points to an underground economy that is unusually large or that has grown rapidly since 1980.

Capital Accumulation

Puerto Rico's economic development has been characterized by an extremely modest rate of domestic saving. In the Puerto Rican national accounts, net household saving has been negative every year since 1957. As discussed earlier, investment has fallen off relative to GDP in recent decades, but remains relatively high as a share of national income. Over the past quarter century, investment has been financed by a combination of capital inflows from the mainland and depreciation accounts. The relatively strong level of corporate saving was undoubtedly influenced by the strong incentives for 936 corporations to reinvest retained earnings in Puerto Rico.

Puerto Rico's apparent lack of private saving is unprecedented, but it is important to recognize that recorded statistics may overstate the problem. If foreign transfer payments to residents of Puerto Rico were underreported, a correction would raise household income and saving and reduce the reported size of the current account deficit. Thus there is a possibility that household saving is understated and foreign saving (the current account deficit) is overstated. This concern is reinforced by the suspension of published information on foreign direct investment in the early 1980s and the inclusion in the balance of payments of a very large residual inflow of unknown transactions. Furthermore, Puerto Rican firms' access to U.S. financial markets mitigates the negative consequences of a low domestic savings rate.

Infrastructure

Bosworth and Collins find significant weakness in Puerto Rico's public infrastructure. Although the Commonwealth has extensive road coverage, it ranks below all but two states in both traffic congestion and surface smoothness. Installed electricity capacity is high, but electricity is also very expensive and there is heavy dependence on petroleum as a source of power.[8] Puerto Rico lags behind other high-income countries in mainline telephones per capita, at only 56 percent of the U.S. level. Puerto Rico looks particularly far behind in new communications and information technologies. Mobile phone use is lower than in some developing economies, such as Chile. Adjusting for population size, Puerto Rico has less than 65 percent the number of Internet users as Chile and less than one-third as many as the mainland. And while there is roughly one secure server per 1,000 Internet users in Ireland, the comparable figure for Puerto Rico is one per 6,000 users. These indicators do not suggest an untapped prowess in information technology, ripe for a sectoral takeoff.

8. Marxuach (2005).

Ireland

As a small island economy connected to a larger market, Ireland offers an intriguing exemplar for Puerto Rico's future growth. Following years of stagnation in the 1980s and early 1990s, the Irish economy grew at 8.5 percent annually in the ten years before 2004 while employment expanded by 50 percent. Although the causes of this turnaround remain in dispute, Bosworth and Collins find a few main factors that may apply to Puerto Rico. First, Ireland benefited from the adoption of a uniform 12.5 percent corporate tax rate in place of a system tilted toward multinationals and filled with exemptions. This experience suggests Puerto Rico can profit from the phase-out of the 936 provisions. Second, the large expansion of employment and the sectoral breadth of those gains were important parts of Irish growth. Ireland has actually reduced the role of capital-intensive activities and achieved rapid growth in a wide range of service industries. Large gains in labor productivity could produce a similar outcome in Puerto Rico.

In his comment, William Baumol emphasized that future growth in Puerto Rico should be based on an information economy. Because Puerto Rico has high wages relative to the rest of Latin America, it must focus future employment growth in areas with commensurately high productivity. Baumol suggests that a lack of vision constitutes the main impediment to such development, characterized by the current gridlock between the two major political parties. José Villamil argued that Puerto Rico should be considered a regional economy for purposes of comparison, rather than a national economy. He also stressed the need for institutional reform as a component of the growth process.

3

Labor Supply and Public Transfers

GARY BURTLESS AND ORLANDO SOTOMAYOR

Puerto Rico's per capita income is less than one-third that of residents on the U.S. mainland. A large part of this gap can be traced to differences between the two economies in the proportion of the population that is employed.[1] And, as shown in figure 3-1, the differences have increased substantially over time. In the immediate postwar period the commonwealth's employment-to-population ratio was 85 to 90 percent of the comparable rate on the mainland. By the early twenty-first century the ratio had fallen to 65 percent.

Burtless and Sotomayor identify four distinct phases in the trend toward lower employment rates on the island relative to those on the mainland. First, the decline in Puerto Rican labor force participation during the 1950s was largely caused by the disappearance of the home needlework industry. In the second period, from the end of the 1950s to the beginning of the 1970s, the employment and labor force participation rates in Puerto Rico remained stable relative to those on the mainland. However, Puerto Rican participation rates fell dramatically relative to those on the mainland between the early 1970s and 1982. The relative participation rate has recovered only modestly from the very depressed levels of the mid-1980s. Currently, in the early

1. Sotomayor (2004).

19

Figure 3-1. *Relative Labor Force Participation and Employment Rates in Puerto Rico Compared with the United States, 1947–2004*[a]

Percent

Source: Authors' estimates using Puerto Rico labor market survey data and U.S. Bureau of Labor Statistics tabulations for the mainland.
a. Civilian population aged sixteen and older.

2000s, the labor force participation rate of Puerto Rican men between twenty and sixty-four years old is just 85 percent of the equivalent participation rate on the U.S. mainland (74 versus 87 percent). This ratio is close to an all-time low for Puerto Rican males. Among women twenty to sixty-four years old, the participation rate in Puerto Rico is only 62 percent of the comparable rate on the U.S. mainland (45 percent versus 72 percent). This is below any comparable ratio attained from the 1950s through the early 1970s.

Burtless and Sotomayor argue that the relatively low participation rates on the island can be explained in part by the generosity and structure of government transfer benefits available to Puerto Rico residents. The rapid expansion of government transfers that occurred during the decade of the 1970s played an important role in discouraging employment and labor force participation on the island, while benefit cuts and eligibility restrictions enacted after 1982 offset only a small part of the adverse effects of earlier benefit expansions, particularly in the food stamp program.

Their conclusions are based on several strands of evidence. First, labor force participation and employment rates fell in Puerto Rico relative to the

Figure 3-2. *Sources of Personal Income, Puerto Rico and the United States, 1950–2004*[a]

Percent (government transfer payments as share of personal income)

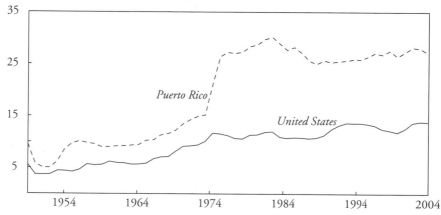

Source: Authors' tabulations of U.S. and Puerto Rican national income and product accounts data.

a. U.S. data are for calendar years; Puerto Rican data are for fiscal years, which begin six months earlier than the corresponding calendar year.

United States immediately after a major expansion in government transfer programs in Puerto Rico in the mid-1970s. Second, participation and employment rates remained depressed long after the economy recovered from the severe recessions of the 1970s and 1980s. Third, the biggest short-falls in Puerto Rican participation rates are observed among population groups with relatively low potential earnings—the young, the old, and women. These are groups where the impact of transfers on behavior should be particularly noticeable: individuals whose potential earnings are below average are the most likely to be eligible for benefits, whether they work or not. In addition, the structure of nearly all benefit formulas provides much more generous income replacement to low-wage than to high-wage workers. Although other developments, including a minimum wage increase and severe recessions after 1973, can account for part of the slump in the Puerto Rican labor supply, it seems clear that changes in the generosity of transfer benefits played a crucial role.

As shown in figure 3-2, government transfer payments account for a large percentage of the total income received by residents of Puerto Rico, and the percentage rose steeply in the 1970s and 1980s. In 1973, govern-ment transfers represented 15 percent of Puerto Rican personal income, compared with 9.5 percent of the personal income received by Americans on the mainland. The introduction of food stamp benefits in Puerto Rico in 1975 dramatically increased the share of personal income derived from transfers. The island's food stamp program was eventually overhauled to reduce costs, but other government benefits grew in size, approximately offsetting the effect of smaller food stamp payments. Since 1990, government transfer benefits have provided 25 percent to 28 percent of Puerto Rico's personal income. This is twice the equivalent percentage on the U.S. mainland.

Because Puerto Rico is the recipient of substantial net transfers from the mainland government, taxpayers on the island do not have to pay for all of the government benefits received by island residents. Low-income Puerto Ricans can enjoy relatively generous income supplements and retirement benefits without imposing heavy tax burdens on highly compensated workers. The transfers received by less affluent citizens depress the incentive for them to work or to migrate to the mainland to find jobs or better wages. Because the commonwealth does not have to pay for all of these transfers, benefits are almost certainly more generous than they would be if island taxpayers had to pay their full cost. As a result, relatively generous redistribution that benefits Puerto Rico's poor, aged, and disabled populations reduces employment rates to below where they would be if all transfers on the island were financed with taxes imposed on Puerto Rico residents.

Burtless and Sotomayor examine in detail the impact of five transfer programs: food stamps, unemployment insurance, Social Security retirement and disability benefits, government-provided health insurance, and Temporary Aid to Needy Families. Each of these programs may have important work-discouraging effects. Even if the effect per dollar spent is no greater in Puerto Rico than in the mainland United States, the effects would still be relatively more important in Puerto Rico because spending is higher in relation to the amount of income island residents can expect to earn in the labor market. There are also reasons to think the proportional effects of the programs are larger in Puerto Rico because so many more of the island's working-age residents are eligible for and receiving benefits. For example, slightly less than 30 percent of Puerto Rican residents receive means-tested nutrition assistance benefits. Participation in the food stamp program on the U.S. mainland is less than one-third as high. Social Security disability payments are provided to island and mainland workers if they are too disabled to work. In principle, similar percentages of U.S. and Puerto Rican adults should become disabled and receive disability payments. In practice, however, disability insurance is relatively more attractive to workers in Puerto Rico than on the mainland, primarily because the benefit formula provides a monthly disability check that replaces a much larger percentage of lost wages on the island than on the mainland.

If Puerto Rico and the mainland of the United States were separate countries, the two nations would have retirement and disability programs that offer distinctly different benefits to workers in the same relative position in their countries' earnings distributions. A male worker earning a wage near the midpoint of the Puerto Rican wage distribution earned about $14,000 in 1999. If he earned a constant wage throughout his career, his Social Security pension would replace 57 percent of his career average earnings. If he were married to someone who earned little throughout her career, his potential monthly pension would replace 86 percent of his career average wages. Obviously, a worker who earns the average Puerto Rican wage qualifies for a pension that replaces a very large percentage of the earnings that would cease if he retired or became disabled. Replacement rates are much lower for typical workers on the mainland. A U.S. male at the midpoint of the mainland wage distribution earned about $32,500 in 1999. His Social Security pension would replace just 43 percent of that amount. Since married women on the mainland are much more likely to have lengthy careers, it is less likely that newly retired married women on the mainland will collect dependent spouse benefits. For workers with a lower earnings rank, the replacement-rate comparison would show an even bigger advantage for workers in Puerto Rico.

Relative Puerto Rican wages have improved since the early 1990s, but they remain 40 percent lower than the average wage earned on the mainland. One reason that wages have grown slowly is that Puerto Ricans accumulate job experience more slowly than their counterparts in the United States. By the time they reach age twenty-five, Puerto Rican men have accumulated almost two fewer years of labor market experience than men of the same age on the U.S. mainland. Twenty-five-year-old Puerto Rican women have accumulated three fewer years of job market experience than their U.S. counterparts. By age forty-five, the deficits in job experience rise to 3.5 years and 7.5 years, respectively, for Puerto Rican men and women. The gap in experience almost certainly carries a penalty in terms of reduced hourly wages. Both education and job experience contribute to worker skills and hence to employers' willingness to pay higher wages. Even though the average educational attainment of Puerto Rican workers has continued to improve relative to schooling attainment on the mainland, Puerto Ricans' average job market experience at successive ages has declined relative to that of mainland residents of the same age.

In view of the generosity of disability insurance pensions for workers who earn low wages, it is not surprising to find that the disability rate in Puerto Rico is well above the U.S. average. Before 1967, participation in the disability insurance program was lower in Puerto Rico than on the mainland, but by 1970 the Puerto Rican rate significantly exceeded the rate in the fifty states. In 1980, Puerto Rico's disability rate was about two and a half times the disability rate on the U.S. mainland. Reforms in the disability insurance program temporarily reduced participation both in Puerto Rico and on the mainland after 1980, but the reforms did not have long-lasting effects. By 2002 the Puerto Rican and nationwide disability rates exceeded their previous peaks, and the Puerto Rican disability rate was almost twice the level on the mainland. This difference may account for 2 to 3 percentage points of the lower labor force participation rate in Puerto Rico compared with the United States. Among older workers, who are most likely to collect a disability insurance check, the difference between Puerto Rican and mainland disability rates is likely to account for an even bigger part of the gap in labor force participation rates.

Puerto Rico's unemployment insurance (UI) program provides benefits that replace only about 26 percent of the average weekly wage in UI-covered employment, substantially less than the replacement rate in the fifty states. Puerto Rico also provides regular UI benefits that have a shorter potential duration than benefits available on the mainland. However, Puerto Rican workers are subject to more frequent layoffs and tend to remain in the program for a longer proportion of the eligible duration. As a result, the program's costs, measured as a percentage of total wages earned in UI-covered employment, are actually higher than on the mainland. In 2000, for example, the average benefit duration of UI claims in Puerto Rico was 18.4 weeks. This is only slightly less than the upper limit on *potential* benefits duration: 20 weeks. On the mainland the average benefit duration was 13.7 weeks, substantially less than the 23.8 weeks of potential benefits that on average were available to a laid-off worker.

The authors conclude that the pattern of insured unemployment reflects the greater difficulty Puerto Rican workers have finding new jobs. However, given the low level of benefits, they argue that this program is unlikely to contribute to the low rate of employment.

Rather than cash, publicly financed health insurance provides an in-kind benefit that provides an important supplement to households' cash incomes. Public health insurance has been expanded in a number of ways, and program expenditures represent about one-fifth of the commonwealth's government tax revenues. Taxes levied to finance the program have an indeterminate effect on the supply of labor. However, the transfer benefits provided by the program unambiguously increase the demand for leisure through an income effect. The provision of free health services to program participants certainly increases their net incomes compared with a no-insurance world, and reduces the need to work in order to obtain insurance from the employer-based system. The work disincentive has probably been enhanced to the extent that the new system (introduced in 1993) provides a higher quantity or quality of services.

The authors supplemented their analysis of the trends in Puerto Rican and mainland transfers and participation rates with detailed analyses of household surveys conducted for the 1970, 1980, 1990, and 2000 censuses. The evidence from the decennial census files shows that a sharply rising fraction of working-age Puerto Ricans collected government transfers during the 1970s and 1980s. In 1969 the percentage of Puerto Rican men who reported that someone in their family collected Social Security benefits was similar to that of mainland U.S. males. After 1969, receiving Social Security benefits became much more common among Puerto Rican men, especially in the lower and middle parts of the earnings distribution. In 1979 and later years about 20 percent of men aged twenty to sixty-four in the second fifth of the male earnings distribution received a Social Security check in Puerto Rico. The comparable percentage of men receiving Social Security on the mainland was only 3 percent.

Participation in Puerto Rican means-tested programs also increased enormously between 1969 and 1989. The comparison with public assistance trends on the mainland is particularly revealing. A far higher proportion of Puerto Ricans in the second and middle fifths of the earnings distribution reported receiving means-tested benefits. Although this was true in 1969, the growth in Puerto Rican participation in means-tested programs after 1969 was very large.

In each of the bottom three-fifths of the male earnings distribution, government transfers represent a much more important source of family income in Puerto Rico than on the mainland. Moreover, the importance of Social Security and assistance income increased sharply after 1969. Mainland men in the second through the top earnings categories derive almost none of their family income from Social Security or public assistance benefits. In contrast, in the second lowest earnings category, transfers accounted for 40 percent of Puerto Rican family income in 1979 and one-third of family income in 1999.

The pattern just described for men is the same for women. In every earnings category, participation in Social Security and public assistance is much

more common among working-age women in the commonwealth than
among women on the mainland. After 1969, participation in transfer programs also rose much faster among Puerto Rican women than it did on the
mainland. Between 1969 and 1999, participation in Social Security
increased from 10 percent to 16 percent of the working-age female population, and participation in means-tested cash public assistance increased from
5 percent to 17 percent of the population. On the U.S. mainland, female
participation rates in transfer programs changed very little over the same
four-decade span. These comparisons suggest that government transfers
have more important practical effects on the labor supply in Puerto Rico
than on the mainland, because transfers are received by a far larger percentage of the working-age population.

Many of the transfer programs are means-tested, meaning that the transfer is reduced when the individual's earned income increases. The nutritional assistance program (NAP), section 8 housing, and the Temporary
Assistance for Needy Families (TANF) programs all base their payments on
the recipient's income. As a result, the increase in net after-tax income from
obtaining a job may be very small for some individuals. The authors present
an example of the situation of a woman with two dependent children who
accepts a job at the minimum wage. If she worked forty hours per week, she
would have monthly earnings of $893. However, after paying the applicable
taxes, losing her TANF and NAP payments, and experiencing a reduction in
housing assistance, her net gain in monthly income would amount to $37.

Figure 3-3 illustrates the implicit tax rate that she would face at various
levels of work effort, ranging from zero to a full-time forty-hour work week.
The tax rate can exceed 100 percent at some critical earnings levels that trig-
ger a reduction or elimination of a transfer payment. But at all levels of the
work week, the effective tax is extraordinarily high and the net income gain
is very small. The authors provide similar examples for higher-earning individuals and the second earner in a two-adult family, but the tax rates are
very similar. Under the current rules, there is no effective economic incentive for recipients of public assistance to seek employment.

Puerto Rican participation rates have been influenced by a number of factors in addition to public transfers. The relative decline in participation and
the currently depressed rate may reflect the increasing size of the informal
sector rather than high levels of economic inactivity. However, the authors
found little evidence that the informal sector is growing faster in Puerto Rico
than it is on the mainland. Migration could also play a role in accounting
for low participation. Puerto Ricans with strong ambitions to advance in the
labor market may move to the mainland, where good jobs are easier to find.

Figure 3-3. *Implicit Tax Rate on Monthly Earnings for a Single Mother in Puerto Rico, 2003*[a]

Percent

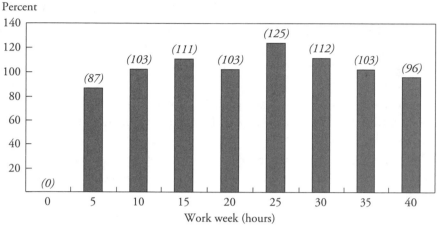

Work week (hours)

Source: Authors' tabulations of data from Puerto Rican public health insurance, TANF, NAP, and section 8 benefit schedules and applicable payroll and commonwealth tax schedules.

a. For women with two children working at the minimum wage. Nonearnings income includes health insurance, TANF, NAP, and section 8 housing subsidies. FICA taxes and income taxes also apply.

Last, there is the issue of the Puerto Rican minimum wage.[2] Although the effects of a high minimum wage on the labor force participation rate are ambiguous, its theoretical impact on the employment rate is straight-forward. If the minimum wage is above the lowest wage that would be negotiated in the absence of regulation, it will reduce the number of jobs offered by employers and eliminate some low-productivity positions. The Puerto Rican minimum wage, like that on the mainland, has risen much more slowly than average wages and productivity since the early 1980s, suggesting that the negative effect on employment has probably declined over the past two decades.

The authors suggest that voters and legislators should aim to increase employment and labor force participation rates on the island so that they approach or match those on the U.S. mainland. To reform social protection programs so that they encourage rather than discourage work, policymakers must consider modifications in current benefit schedules and new eligibility rules for assistance.

One feature of programs that encourage work is that they target benefits on people who become employed or on workers who boost their monthly or

2. See Castillo-Freeman and Freeman (1992) and Krueger (1995) for details on the minimum wage in Puerto Rico.

annual hours of work. An example of such a program is the earned income tax credit (EITC) in the United States. The program provides a type of transfer known as an earnings subsidy. It offers jobless adults a powerful incentive to become employed. The subsidy tops up the earnings a worker receives from his employer with a supplement that is equal to some percentage of his wages. People who do not work are not eligible to receive the earnings subsidy. An earnings subsidy boosts recipients' net incomes, just like any other transfer program. But for many low-wage workers, it raises rather than reduces the reward for work by increasing the recipient's net wage.

In contrast, a typical assistance program, such as Puerto Rico's Nutritional Assistance Program (NAP), discourages its recipients from working. By providing generous benefits to working-age adults who are jobless, the NAP reduces the need to work. By offering benefits that shrink as recipients' own labor incomes rise, the program reduces the net income payoff that workers derive from working more hours.

A compelling argument in favor of plans like the EITC is that they can increase the employment rates and net incomes of participating families without causing a sizable reduction in their own self-support. In comparison with other methods of reducing the tax burdens or raising the transfer benefits of the working poor, the EITC offers a strong inducement to work, has positive effects on the earned incomes of people who earn the lowest wages, and has a relatively small work disincentive effect on people in the phase-out range of the benefit schedule.[3]

From a taxpayer's perspective, however, an earnings supplement in Puerto Rico would represent a costly new commitment to redistribution in behalf of the poor. Burtless and Sotomayor suggest two steps to ensure that overall spending on transfer payments does not increase when stronger work incentives are introduced into the system. First, they propose that any Puerto Rican wage supplement program should require participating workers to hold jobs that meet minimum hours conditions. For example, to receive a wage supplement, a family could be required to have at least one breadwinner who works no fewer than thirty hours a week. By restricting supplements to breadwinners who work nearly full-time, larger subsidy payments could be paid to workers who make the biggest increases in the number of hours they work a month. This restriction will simultaneously reduce costs, by eliminating payments to people with short work weeks, and encourage jobless workers to take jobs with longer work weeks. A

---

3. For a discussion of an EITC in the Puerto Rican context, see Enchautegui (2003).

second step toward restraining transfer costs would be to reduce NAP benefits currently payable to able-bodied working-age adults. One possible
reform would place time limits on NAP benefits payable to such adults.
This measure would increase the incentive for jobless recipients of NAP to
find a job. At the same time, the budget savings realized from this reform
could be used to finance an earnings supplement program.

In her discussion Eileen Segarra argued that too much emphasis was given
to the role of the transfer programs. She pointed out that they had been
scaled back in recent years with little discernible effect on labor force participation. She stressed that demand-side factors as reflected in the high
level of unemployment discourage entry into the labor market. She also
argued that cultural factors account for much of the difference in labor
force participation between women in Puerto Rico and women on the
mainland. Katherine Terrell also felt that too large a role was assigned to
transfers as the source of the low participation rate. In her view, the large
difference in average incomes between the mainland United States and
Puerto Rico could distort some of the comparison of the frequency of
reliance on the transfer programs. She suggested that it would be fruitful to
concentrate on a comparison with the poorest of the U.S. states.

4

Why Don't More Puerto Rican Men Work? The Rich Uncle (Sam) Hypothesis

MARÍA E. ENCHAUTEGUI AND RICHARD B. FREEMAN

María Enchautegui and Richard Freeman also focus their chapter on Puerto Rico's strikingly low employment rate. In 2000, only 31 percent of the population was employed, giving the island the lowest employment-to-population ratio in the Americas and Caribbean, if not in the world. The low employment rate compromises the island's development by diverting resources from possible investment to public assistance and services to the large nonworking population. Their analysis focuses on men because they find that it is the low employment rate for men that is "off the map" in comparison with that in other countries.

The discussion is organized around what the authors call the "rich uncle (Sam) hypothesis." A rich uncle is a wealthy relative who provides resources to poorer relatives for consumption and employs other resources for production. The rich uncle reduces incentives for relatives to work and lowers the demand for their services as well. In this sense, the connection of the relatively poor economy of Puerto Rico to the advanced and rich economy of the United States has created conditions that support low employment.

Male Labor Force Participation and Employment

Puerto Rico's male participation rate stood at approximately 57.7 percent throughout the period 2000–2003. As shown in figure 4-1, this is a very low percentage in comparison with the participation rate in numerous countries in the Caribbean and the rest of the world. Although the female participation rate throughout the same period was lower (35 percent), it is comparable to that in some countries, including Italy, Chile, and Argentina. Over time, moreover, the participation rate of men in Puerto Rico has fallen while female participation has increased. Data collected from the household labor force surveys indicate that from 1971 to 2003, the gap in labor force participation between the mainland United States and Puerto Rico increased twice as much for men (67 percent) as for women (33 percent). These trends also mean that by 2003 the mainland U.S. *female* participation rate stood close to the Puerto Rican *male* participation rate.

In a comparison by age group, from 1970 to 1999, participation among Puerto Rican men fell more among older men than among younger men. Similarly, during the same period, at all education levels, the labor force participation rate of men in Puerto Rico was below that of men in the mainland United States. The Puerto Rico–mainland U.S. employment gap is highest among high school graduates and lowest among bachelor's degree holders.

The annual work activity of employed men shows only modest variations, which in certain instances can be attributed to differences in how some workers report weeks worked. Nevertheless, the big differences are in the proportion of nonworking men who worked in the previous five years. Whereas just 35 percent of Puerto Rican men out of the labor force reported having worked in the previous five years, 68 percent of men out of the labor force on the mainland reported having worked in the previous five years.[1] The authors document that this is not the result of any huge difference in the age distribution of the two populations, but rather reflects the relatively permanent detachment of a large number of Puerto Rican men from the workforce.

In Puerto Rico, the principal reported activity of women who are not in the labor force was working at home.[2] For men, the principal reported reason for being out of the labor force was disability. Between 1990 and 2000, the proportion of men who reported being disabled jumped from 16.4 percent to 25.6 percent. By contrast, most women out of the labor force are engaged in household work; less than 3 percent report themselves as disabled.

1. United States Census 2000 and Puerto Rico Census 2000.
2. Estado Libre Asociado de Puerto Rico (2002).

Figure 4-1. *Labor Force Participation Rate, Men and Women, Selected Countries, 2000–03*

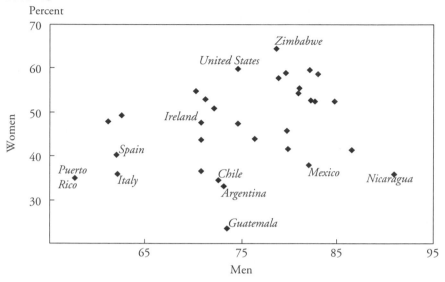

Source: Data from International Labor Organization, online statistics (lasborsta.ilo.org [May 2005]).

In sum, diverse measures of labor force activity derived from the census and household surveys show that Puerto Rican men had exceptionally low labor market participation at the turn of the twenty-first century. This result reflects a downward trend in participation in the 1970s that produced a permanent detachment of many men from the workforce and a rising proportion who reported themselves as disabled in the 1990s.

Factors Contributing to Low Participation Rates

Enchautegui and Freeman identify and examine a number of interacting factors that may have played a role. One of these is the distorted relationship between aggregate demand and employment. Since the implementation of the 936 code of the federal internal revenue system in Puerto Rico in the late 1970s, gross national production and gross domestic production have diverged. The ratio of GNP to GDP in Puerto Rico fell from 0.93 in 1970 to 0.74 in 1985 to 0.67 in 1997, which means that GDP grew much more rapidly than GNP. To the extent that GDP does not accurately measure production on the island, employment should be more closely related to the slower-growing GNP than to the faster-growing GDP. The authors' analyses indicate that aggregate economic growth in Puerto Rico was less favorable to employment than first appears to be the case because it took the form of GDP growth that is not part of GNP. Furthermore, the pattern of GDP and employment in Puerto Rico may have been distorted by its close relationship with the U.S. mainland and the tax incentives for investing in capital-intensive activities, primarily through section 936 of the tax law.

Second, like Burtless and Sotomayor, they argue that transfer programs play an important role. In 2003, island residents received $14.3 billion in transfers, mostly from the federal government. The total amount transferred from U.S. coffers to island citizens implies a huge proportionate transfer payment from one economy to another, with potentially large impacts on the labor supply.

The major federally funded transfer program in Puerto Rico is Old Age, Survivors, Disability, and Insurance (OASDI). A larger proportion of OASDI spending in Puerto Rico consists of disability payments than in the United States. Administrative data from the Social Security Administration show that 19 percent of Puerto Rican Social Security beneficiaries were receiving disability payments, in comparison with 12 percent of U.S. Social Security beneficiaries. In addition, almost one in ten adult men in Puerto Rico under the age of sixty-five receives Social Security income. The comparable figure for the mainland United States is one in twenty. Among men aged forty-six to sixty-four, 22 percent receive this type of income. The potential for disability insurance to discourage work in Puerto Rico is enormous, considering the low earnings of Puerto Rican workers and the high levels of unemployment. In 2002, support for disabled workers in Puerto Rico was $713 per month—80 percent of the $891 monthly payment to disabled workers on the mainland. Similarly, both retirement benefits and wages (including fringe benefits) in Puerto Rico are about two-thirds the size of those in the mainland United States.

Another component of federal transfers to Puerto Rico is the Nutritional Assistance Program (NAP), which is the most widespread government assistance program on the island. The Puerto Rican NAP benefits differ from the U.S. food stamp program. NAP has high implicit tax rates and covers a huge proportion of the workforce, in contrast to the low implicit marginal tax rates on the U.S. food stamp program and its limited coverage of the population. NAP, rather than Temporary Assistance for Needy Families, is the main government assistance program in Puerto Rico. The Department of the Family reports about half a million "units" on NAP.

Taken together, the Social Security disability program and the NAP program combined could have large effects on male employment. Unfortunately, there are no data rich enough in Puerto Rico to sort out these effects.

Nonetheless, the authors attempt to draw some inferences about the potential effect of nonwork income on labor supply from data on the work patterns of married couples.

To determine the work patterns of married couples, they matched wife and husband records for persons aged eighteen to sixty-four from the 2000 Puerto Rican census and tabulated the employment status of both spouses. In 36 percent of the cases both the wife and husband were without work. This figure suggests Puerto Rico has an extraordinarily high proportion of "jobless families."[3] While it is not possible given the data at hand to estimate how many of the husbands in the "jobless families" are not working because their families receive income from transfers, the large percentage of couples in this category suggests that the effects of transfers on male employment could be quite large. Families with no earners must be making money in some fashion. With about half of Puerto Rican families receiving NAP support and many men obtaining disability insurance, it appears likely that many of the jobless families are recipients of either or both of these forms of income, depressing their incentive to work, at least in the formal sector.

A third potential factor arises from the option for workers to migrate to the mainland. Given that residents of Puerto Rico are U.S. citizens, migration can affect the employment-population and labor participation ratios in Puerto Rico. First, if unemployed persons were to leave the island to seek work on the mainland, the employment rate in Puerto Rico would rise because the number of persons of working age would decline. Second, migration could reduce the labor participation rate through selectivity if those persons with strong attachment to the labor market are more likely to migrate to the mainland. The migration of those who want to work but do not have jobs would lower the labor force proportionately more than it would lower the population. Third, migration could affect employment and participation indirectly by raising the reservation wages of persons on the island. Since migration gives Puerto Ricans access to higher-wage U.S. jobs, some persons might set their reservation wages on the basis of what they could get working on the mainland, producing a lower bound on wages that could be too high to accommodate excess labor.

Enchautegui and Freeman use census data on the employment of Puerto Rican–born men residing in Puerto Rico and of those residing as migrants on the mainland United States to assess the *maximum* contribution that selective migration could make to the low employment rate in Puerto Rico. The main findings are reported in table 4-1. The first line shows the proportion of men

3. Gregg and Wadsworth (2001).

Table 4-1. *Emigration and Employment Rates, Puerto Rican Men, Puerto Rico and the United States, by Education, 2000*[a]

Percent

| Category | Educational attainment | | | | |
	To eleven years	Twelve years	Thirteen to fifteen years	Sixteen or more years	All
Emigration rate	45	37	26	27	37
Employed in Puerto Rico	32	48	54	72	46
Employed in the United States	43	61	70	84	55
Simulated employed in Puerto Rico[b]	37	53	58	75	49
Difference					
Employed in the United States minus employed in Puerto Rico	11	13	16	12	9
Puerto Ricans employed in Puerto Rico, simulated minus actual	5	5	4	3	3

Source: Data from Ruggles and others (2004); and U.S. Census Bureau, 5% Public Use Microdata Sample, 2000 Census of Population for Puerto Rico; authors' tabulations.

a. Persons eighteen to sixty-four years of age.

b. The simulation assumes that all migrants return to Puerto Rico and are employed at the same rate as in the United States.

aged eighteen or older who were born in Puerto Rico but reside on the mainland. This emigration rate is much higher for those with less education, reflecting a long-standing pattern of reverse brain drain. The authors simulate what the male employment rate in Puerto Rico would be if immigrants returned to the island but had the same employment rate as on the mainland. As shown in line 6, their estimates for different educational categories range from 3 to 5 percentage points above the actual Puerto Rican employment rates. This suggests that selective migration is a modest factor in the low employment rate on the island.

Fourth, the authors focus on Puerto Rico's wage structure. From the perspective of labor demand analysis, low employment suggests an imbalance in the level and pattern of wages. Are wages too high relative to the level of economic development of Puerto Rico? Is the structure of wages by skill inconsistent with the supply of skills? If so, part of the island's employment problem could be associated with wage levels and patterns inconsistent with the levels necessary to clear the labor market.

To explore these issues, they compare earnings in Puerto Rico with earnings in the fifty United States and in the state with the lowest per capita income, Mississippi. For production workers in manufacturing, the hourly pay or labor costs (including fringe benefits) is about two-thirds of the hourly pay or labor costs in the mainland United States. Puerto Rican production workers in manufacturing earn 81–85 percent of the hourly pay or labor costs of their counterparts in Mississippi. Since living expenses in the two places are comparable, these figures indicate differences in real earnings.[4] The data for the hourly earnings of all workers show a bigger gap between Puerto Rico, the mainland United States, and Mississippi. Puerto Ricans earn 59 percent of the earnings of workers on the mainland and 74–79 percent of the earnings of workers in Mississippi, depending on whether earnings are given as medians or means.[5]

Decomposing the data by education reveals that, in comparison with the mainland United States, relative earnings for both men and women on the island are highest among the most educated and among the least educated. In comparison with earnings in Mississippi, the relative earnings of men on the island are highest for the most educated. For women the relative earnings are highest for the least educated. Thus the authors' analysis demonstrates that, overall, the highest relative earnings are for less educated workers. This is quite surprising because the normal pattern in earnings differences among countries with different levels of income is that earnings in a lower-income economy are closer to earnings in a higher-income economy among the most educated or skilled.[6]

To see whether the pattern of relatively high earnings among low-paid workers holds across occupations, the authors compared earnings by occupation in Puerto Rico and Mississippi. The data show that earnings in Puerto Rico are higher than in Mississippi in the selected occupations at the top of the earnings distribution; they are markedly lower for the occupations in the middle of the distribution; and they are relatively close for occupations with low earnings. Other calculations were performed to see if the pattern of relatively high wages at the top and bottom of the earnings distribution holds, with similar results.

The combination of relatively high wages at the bottom of the earnings distribution together with high joblessness is puzzling. The natural question to ask is why the high joblessness in Puerto Rico has not driven wages down at the bottom of the wage distribution to create more jobs. The rich uncle hypothesis suggests three possible answers.

---

4. Bosworth and Collins (2006), appendix A.
5. Freeman and Enchautegui (2006), table 4-9.
6. Freeman and Oostendorp (2002).

On the demand side, it is possible that Puerto Rico's adoption of the U.S. minimum wage limited downward wage adjustments.[7] Since Puerto Rico has lower productivity and average wages than the mainland United States, the minimum affects a larger proportion of the workforce than it does in the United States. Because the federal minimum rate was constant at $5.15 per hour from 1997 through 2004, it limited annual earnings of full-time workers on the island to about $10,700 per year. This level is below the earnings for several low-wage occupations and indeed falls below the mean earnings in the lowest decile of the Puerto Rican earnings distribution: $13,399 for a sample of 538 occupations. The minimum wage may affect the lower part of the wage distribution, but given this large gap the authors conclude that other factors are more important. A second possible reason for the relatively high level of wages for low-paying occupations in Puerto Rico is that income transfers have created a reservation wage considerably above the minimum and above the full-employment wage rates.

The third possible reason for a high reservation wage on the island is that potential migration to the United States creates a floor for wages above the minimum. Arguably, if migrants returned to Puerto Rico, they would increase the labor supply and drive down the wage, which would raise employment. However, this would not necessarily raise the *rate of employment*, which would change depending on how much wages fell and the elasticity of demand to labor. The authors describe a simple stylized model where the potential for migration to the higher-wage mainland sets a lower bound on wages in Puerto Rico, which depresses employment there. What makes the lower employment tolerable is the existence of diverse social benefits for persons on the island paid for by the mainland, the option to migrate to the United States to earn higher wages, and the potential to make money outside of the formal sector.

Measuring the Impact of the Informal Sector

There is a widespread belief that many jobless Puerto Rican men work in the informal sector, which standard labor force surveys fail to measure. In Puerto Rico, the informal labor market could provide job opportunities for men who cannot find work in the formal labor market while allowing them to receive government benefits such as NAP and disability insurance, which are work-tested or means-tested, that they would lose if they took formal sector jobs.

7. Castillo-Freeman and Freeman (1992); Krueger (1995).

For the informal sector to explain the low level of labor participation in Puerto Rico, it must be a large share of the economy. Some studies estimate that it accounts for upwards of 23 percent of the GDP of Puerto Rico.[8] For the informal sector to explain the declining participation and employment population rate in Puerto Rico, however, it would have to have grown since the 1970s, on which the evidence is not as clear.

Standard labor force data provide indirect evidence on the possible size and development of informal sector work. One natural indicator of the informal sector is the proportion of workers who are self-employed. Since 1980 the proportion of self-employed reported by the Department of Labor in Puerto Rico has fluctuated between 11 and 12 percent, or about 5 points above the 6–7 percent who are self-employed in the mainland United States. Since the self-employed are counted as workers, these figures do not measure non-labor-force participants who work in the informal sector. Another indicator of the potential level and growth of the informal sector is the proportion of men who are out of the labor force, not disabled, not going to school, and not doing housework. These men may be idle, but they could just as readily be informal sector workers since they have no other reported activity and have no reported physical or other impediments to work. The proportion of men in this category declined from 1970 to 2000.

Despite the appeal of the informal sector hypothesis as a contributor to the low participation rate of Puerto Rican men, there has been no direct study of workers involved in this sector. To fill this gap, the authors undertook a pilot survey in the summer of 2004 to find out what men in communities with potentially low employment were doing. They randomly selected men in households from low-to-medium-income communities along El Caño Martín Peña in the capital city of San Juan. They interviewed 133 men drawn from households containing men aged eighteen to sixty-four not attending school. As shown in table 4-2, the survey suggests that the official Department of Labor questionnaire understates employment considerably but understates labor force participation only modestly. Since the survey covered a group of men that had a relatively high rate of employment and participation even by the Department of Labor standard, it is possible that the understatement, particularly of labor participation, would be larger in a more representative sample. The results suggest that informal sector work helps explain a significant part of the low employment rate of Puerto Rican men, but can explain only 3 or so percentage points of their low participation rate.

8. Pol (2004); Estudios Técnicos (2004).

Table 4-2. *Labor Force Activity according to Pilot Survey and Household Survey,
Men, Selected Puerto Rican Communities, 2004*
Units as indicated

Activity	Number	Share of sample (percent)
N for pilot survey	133	100.0
According to household survey question		
Working, traditional work	94	71.0
Not working but looking for work (unemployed)	11	8.0
Working or unemployed (in labor force)	105	79.0
According to pilot survey question		
Reporting nontraditional work	29	22.0
Reporting nontraditional work but reported not working on household survey question	15	11.0
Reporting nontraditional work but reported neither working nor looking for work on household survey question	5	4.0
All working, including the fifteen nontraditional workers who reported they were not working on household survey	109	82.0
Reporting participating in the labor force, including nontraditional employed	110	83.0

Source: Data from Encuesta de Empleo y Uso del Tiempo–El Caño and authors' calculations.

Summing Up

Enchautegui and Freeman's analysis shows that a variety of factors contributed to the low employment rate of Puerto Rican men. The common thread behind these separate factors, which they have termed the rich uncle hypothesis, is that Puerto Rico's low employment rate stems from its unique relationship with the mainland United States, which has produced an economic environment that discourages work on both the supply and demand sides of the market. The rich uncle hypothesis suggests that the close tie between the island and the mainland has been a double-edged relation, offering Puerto Ricans many of the benefits of living in a highly advanced economy but also contributing to the employment problem. The authors conclude that there are advantages to having a rich uncle, but as anyone with rich relatives knows, it is a mixed blessing.

The chapter ends with a discussion of policy implications derived from the analysis. It is the federal—not the Puerto Rican—government that controls many of the factors that affect employment. These include the level of benefits of Social Security and eligibility into this program, the minimum wage, federal tax incentives, the amount of transfers to the poor, and border control. The authors argue that Puerto Rico needs to work with the U.S. government to redesign these programs to be more work-friendly, which would help to reduce poverty on the island. Puerto Rico could seek ways to make support of low-income persons more compatible with employment, for instance through an earned income tax credit arrangement or tax credits to firms on the basis of the number of jobs created.

Nongovernmental organizations could try to combine their services to the low-income population with employment. Work activities common to the informal labor market such as construction and reparation work could be organized through cooperatives of community workers or through community organizations, bringing these workers out of the shadows of informality. Since much of the low participation of men occurs among older men, perhaps a shift in compensation toward deferred benefits such as pensions or health insurance would reduce the rate of withdrawal from the workforce. The goal should be to link benefits to work rather than to nonwork, to induce adult men not in the workforce or doing informal work into regular jobs, and raise Puerto Rico from its current position at the bottom of country and area tables of male employment and labor participation rates.

In her comments on this study, Belinda Reyes began by questioning the timing of the rise in transfer payments and the decline in labor force participation. She noted that as a share of the U.S. employment rate the Puerto Rican rate began to decline in the late 1950s, while the sharp rise in transfer payments did not occur until the 1970s. Reyes also put forth some alternative reasons for the abnormally high proportion of older Puerto Rican men claiming disability insurance. For example, 48,000 Puerto Ricans served in the Vietnam War, and many of those were part of the forty-six to sixty-four age cohort in the 2000 census. Finally, Reyes drew attention to some possible explanators of the low labor force participation rate not accounted for by the rich uncle hypothesis. The role of the Puerto Rican government as the largest employer on the island, the strong union presence, and the substantial undocumented immigrant flows *into* Puerto Rico all could explain some of the peculiar features of the Puerto Rican labor market.

5

Education and Economic Development

HELEN F. LADD AND FRANCISCO L. RIVERA-BATIZ

In this chapter, Ladd and Rivera-Batiz review Puerto Rico's remarkable record of educational development over the past forty years—one that is surpassed by few countries in the world. Moreover, this educational expansion has contributed significantly to the economic development of the island. Despite its accomplishments, they argue that the Puerto Rican education system currently faces serious challenges. Significant increases in the quality of schooling are necessary for the island to continue to use education as an engine of economic development. The problem of large educational inequities among different social groups also deserves close attention.

Growth of the Education Sector

Starting in the mid-1940s, the government committed itself to raising the educational attainment of Puerto Rico's population. To this end, between 1944 and 1962, public spending on education quadrupled in real terms and has continued to expand at both the school and university levels until the present time. The result was dramatically rising student enrollments. As of 2000, census data indicate that the net enrollment rate of children in elementary school (ages six to twelve) was 98.8 percent, and in secondary education (ages thirteen to eighteen) it was 91.3 percent. A similar expansion

Figure 5-1. *Educational Attainment of Adult Population, Puerto Rico,*
Selected Years, 1940–2000[a]
Years of schooling

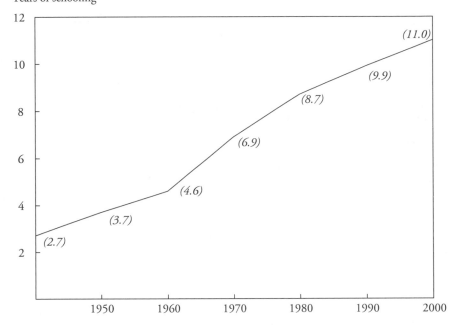

Source: U.S. Census of Population for Puerto Rico, various years.
a. Persons aged twenty-five and older.

occurred at the tertiary level, where enrollment rose from 12,600 students
in 1950–51 to over 200,000 today.

The sharp increase in enrollment rates has led to a rapid rise in educational attainment (see figure 5-1). The average years of schooling of Puerto
Rican workers increased from 2.7 years in 1940 to 11.0 years in 2000 and
are now comparable to that of the mainland United States and many other
high-income countries such as France, Denmark, Great Britain, Finland,
and Ireland. It also exceeds that of the most educated Latin American
nations, such as Chile, Argentina, Peru, and Uruguay.

By 2000, 18.2 percent of the population twenty-five and older had a college degree or more, up from only 3.5 percent in 1960.[1] If the adults who
attended some college are added to those who received a degree, the proportion doubles. These figures place Puerto Rico in the top tier of world
nations ranked by their proportion of college-educated adults. As of 2000,

1. Based on the analysis of data from U.S. Department of Commerce (2003) and earlier census
data files.

the United States tops the list with 28 percent of adults aged twenty-five to sixty-four with a college degree. Puerto Rico's 20.2 percent puts it below Norway and the Netherlands, but above or tied with all other OECD countries and well above developing countries with equivalent levels of per capita income. The authors' analysis of 2000 census data shows that the proportion of college graduates in Puerto Rico also exceeds the proportion of Puerto Ricans in the United States with a college degree, which was 13.4 percent for the population aged twenty-five to sixty-four.

Concerns about School Quality and Social Inequities

Though Puerto Rico's progress in raising the average quantity of schooling is beyond dispute, less clear is what has been happening to the quality of education, especially since the early 1990s. Ladd and Rivera-Batiz point out that evaluating student achievement is made difficult by the limited availability of systematic testing in schools until the mid-1990s. Even then, the implementation of school-wide testing occurred only gradually, and the tests cannot be compared over time since they changed from year to year.

The only achievement data available over time are for high school students who take the battery of tests included in the College Board University Admissions and Assessment Program. This Puerto Rican equivalent of the SAT is designed for high school students applying to colleges and universities in Puerto Rico. It includes an aptitude test with verbal and quantitative components, and achievement tests in English, Spanish, and mathematics. Average scores on these tests have failed to rise over time and even generally dropped after the mid-1990s, with the biggest declines on the math and Spanish achievement tests. However, because the number and composition of students taking these exams has changed over time, their value for measuring changes in educational quality is limited.

An alternative way to judge how well the public school system is meeting the educational needs of its students is to look at the rates at which students are switching to private schools. Private schools are increasingly the schools of choice for those who can afford them in Puerto Rico. As a result, the private sector has grown from a relatively small sector providing elite education to a small proportion of the population to a much larger and diverse system serving 25 percent of all students (see table 5-1). As the more able and more motivated students leave, it becomes increasingly difficult for the public system to keep its test scores from falling and to convince families that public schools are not deteriorating, which leads to another round of departures; and the cycle continues. These trends illustrate the bifurcation of the educa-

Table 5-1. *School Enrollment, Puerto Rico, Selected Years, 1940–2003*[a]

School year	Public	Private	Total	Private as share of total (percent)
1940	286,098	12,374	298,472	4.1
1950	416,206	25,552	441,758	6.1
1960	573,440	63,300	636,740	9.9
1970	686,770	89,106	775,870	11.5
1980	712,880	98,500	811,380	12.1
1990	644,734	145,800	790,534	18.7
2000	607,626	163,946	771,572	21.2
2003	565,763	185,745	751,508	24.7

Source: Data from Rivera-Batiz (1993); Commonwealth of Puerto Rico (1994, 1996a, 1998, 2000, 2004a).

a. Fall enrollment in public and private primary and secondary schools and public prekindergarten and kindergarten programs.

tion system and do not bode well for the long-term health of the island's public school system.

Equally worrisome is the fact that private schools themselves are of widely varying quality, with the academic standards of some of the new ones being far below those of the more established elite private schools. Although private schools must request and periodically renew a license from the General Council of Education, the renewal process does not require a significant academic review. The General Council of Education accredits schools, but only at the request of the institution. To be sure many private schools are accredited by U.S.-based accreditation organizations or have their own accountability systems. However, there is currently no mechanism for public monitoring of the quality of private schools.

The public school system is perceived to have extremely high dropout rates. However, the authors find that about 21 percent of the persons aged eighteen to twenty-four who are not still enrolled in high school do not have a high school credential. Though significantly higher than the comparably estimated dropout rate of 16.5 percent for the mainland United States, the 21 percent is far lower than the 40–50 percent rates that have been cited for Puerto Rico in the past.

At the same time, dropout rates for students from low-income families are still very high: about 37 percent on average for students from poor families. Adding those youth aged eighteen to twenty-four who were still in school, 48.2 percent of youth from low-income families were experiencing significant schooling delays or had dropped out all together. That statistic suggests a cycle of poverty and poor schooling that would need to be broken for the island to increase in any significant way the income and education of its most disadvantaged populations.

The Failure of Policy Initiatives Related to Schools

In 1990, Puerto Rico began a major overhaul of its education system designed to decentralize the Department of Education, which had tightly controlled all areas of public schooling. The initial law introduced an administrative layer of local school districts and school-based councils designed to foster the input of parents, teachers, students, and community members. That law was extended by the Community Schools Development Act of 1993 and then was replaced by the 1999 Organic Law that currently governs the system. This law formally placed community schools at the center of the system, gave them more authority, and reassigned functions and powers to ten regions and eighty-four school districts.

In addition to these governance changes, during the 1990s Puerto Rico significantly increased its public spending on elementary and secondary education. As a result, by 2003, spending per student had risen to $4,145, about double its level in 1990 and more than triple its level in 1970. Despite this sharp increase in spending, however, Puerto Rico still spent only about half the U.S. average per pupil and significantly less than Utah and Mississippi, the two lowest-spending states.[2] Nonetheless, Puerto Rico is making an unusually large effort in public education by U.S. and world standards. Based on the standard measure of education effort—spending on primary and secondary education (from own sources) per student as a percentage of GNP per capita—figure 5-2 shows that Puerto Rico's share of 25 percent exceeded the U.S. average of 22 percent and is far above comparable shares for Argentina, Ireland, and Mexico. Similarly, as a share of the commonwealth's general fund budget in 2002–03, primary and secondary education expenditures were 20.1 percent of all government expenses. This share far exceeds that in most other countries. For example, in 2000 elementary and secondary education spending as a proportion of total government expenditures was 14.4 percent in the Republic of Korea, 10.3 percent in Denmark, 7.1 percent in Ireland, 9.2 percent in Spain, 15.2 percent in Chile, 10.9 percent in Argentina, and 9.4 percent in Uruguay.

The new spending partly financed the hiring of new teachers, leading to a reduction in the number of pupils per teacher from 20.4 in 1988–89 to 15.4 in 2003–04. Though teacher salaries rose in current dollars, the base

2. National Center for Education Statistics (2003).

Figure 5-2. *Public Spending on K-12 Education per Student as Percent of GNP per Capita, Selected Countries*
Percent

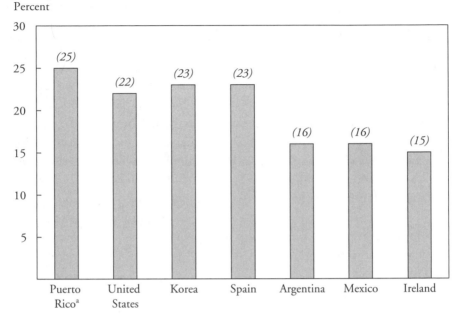

Source: OECD (2003); Commonwealth of Puerto Rico (2004a).
a. Excludes U.S. (federal) government spending on education.

salary in real terms remained lower in 2003 than in the late 1960s, and well below that on the mainland. The average starting salary of a teacher in Puerto Rico (with a bachelor's degree) was $18,000 in 2002–03, the equivalent of a base salary of $1,500 per month. By comparison, the average starting salary in the United States was $29,564, or $2,464 per month.

Unfortunately, the governance reforms and spending increases have not yielded the desired results, a problem that Ladd and Rivera-Batiz attribute to poor implementation.[3] (The initial governance reforms were top-down with no buy-in from stakeholders such as teachers; they were introduced too abruptly into a school system that was unprepared for the massive administrative shifts they entailed; and the new funding led to corruption at the highest levels of the Department of Education. Because the new institutional structures did not materialize in practice, the island's 1,500 schools continue to report directly to the secretary of education, but are also now subject to several layers of authority that embody different and often conflicting approaches and mandates.

3. Commonwealth of Puerto Rico Department of Education (2003 and 2004).

The Department of Education is by far the largest agency within the government of Puerto Rico. Between 1988–89 and 2003–04, the number of nonclassroom staff per 100 classroom staff rose from 86.7 to 88.5. Though the number of administrative staff per 100 classroom staff declined from 33.5 to 28.0 during the period, this decline reflects the large increase in classroom teachers. If administrators are measured relative to students, the story changes: That indicator rises from 16.4 in 1988–89 to 18.2 in 2003–04. The figures for the United States as a whole and New York (a state not known for its bureaucratic leanness) are substantially lower.

The authors argue that the lack of accountability is a severe systemwide problem. The student assessment component of the reforms has become operational only in the past few years. Accountability at the school level is nonexistent, with both student and teacher absenteeism a common problem. A recent study documents that, among both groups, the average level of absenteeism is equivalent to five weeks of classes during the academic year.[4]

What Next for the Schooling Sector?

The failure of the past fifteen years of reform to increase achievement levels and to keep students in the public schools poses a serious challenge for the island. Ladd and Rivera-Batiz argue that the system now faces the worst of both worlds: a large and politicized bureaucracy and a failed program to give more authority to individual schools, with little or no accountability at either level.

The authors argue that Puerto Rico must continue with the policy of decentralization in an effort to make the system work better. However, they doubt that giving more authority to schools will, by itself, generate higher achievement. Nor will it reduce educational disparities among schools. They point instead to the importance of providing support services to the schools that need them the most and of recognizing that some schools may need alternative governance arrangements.

With respect to accountability, Puerto Rico is now subject to the test-based accountability provisions of the No Child Left Behind Act of 2001 and therefore must test all students annually in grades 3–8 and measure their progress toward the goal of 100 percent proficiency by 2014. While some parts of the legislation should be helpful to Puerto Rico, the authors are concerned that the failure of many low-performing schools to meet

4. Castillo Ortiz and Marrero (2003, p. 28).

annual performance standards could further discredit the public school system and lead to a greater movement of students to the private sector.

The government will have to work hard to avoid these negative consequences while at the same time seizing the opportunity to develop a more
reasonable and constructive accountability system. Such a system would be
based on value-added measures of school effectiveness, would include support for failing schools and provide substantial funds for improved quality of
teaching. In addition, it will require a more dynamic and cost-effective
leadership at all levels of the school system. It should also seek a greater
integration of schools into social and community service programs designed
to improve family economic well-being and promote parental involvement.

Higher Education and the Labor Market
Consequences of Schooling

Tertiary education enrollments in Puerto Rico have risen sharply. However, Ladd and Rivera-Batiz point out that only 39 percent of the students currently enrolled in higher education are male. Though there are
good economic reasons for women to invest more heavily in higher education than men, the sharply declining proportion of males attending college is a matter of concern. On a long-term basis, the prospects of creat-
ing an underclass of Puerto Rican men whose lack of college education
prevents entry into mainstream labor markets may have profound social
implications.

Though the initial expansion of tertiary education was primarily in the
public sector, enrollment in the private institutions has been growing more
rapidly. It overtook enrollment in the University of Puerto Rico (UPR)—
the only public institution of higher education—in the mid-1970s and now
accounts for 62.7 percent of all students in college. Some of the UPR cam-
puses have been more selective in their admissions than private institutions.
As a result, the public sector tends to cater to the more affluent layers of
Puerto Rican society while the private sector enrolls a high proportion of
students from less affluent backgrounds. But Puerto Rican public universities rely far less heavily on tuition and fees than public institutions on the
mainland. In contrast to the 18.1 percent of spending that is financed by
tuition and fees in the United States, only 7.2 percent is financed that way
in Puerto Rico. The result is a perverse distributional pattern that exacer-
bates income differences on the island.

The authors argue that the island's public universities should rely on
higher tuition and fees for those families that can afford them, combined

Figure 5-3. *Public Spending on Higher Education per Student, Puerto Rico, Selected Years, 1975–2003*[a]

Constant dollars (2003)

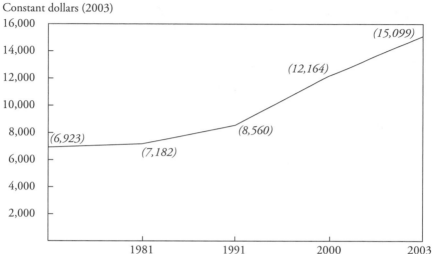

Source: National Center for Education Statistics (2004; 2003, p. 379, table 337).
a. Data for University of Puerto Rico system only.

with scholarships for those who cannot. In the United States, the average annual tuition and fees for four-year institutions was $3,746 in 2001–02; the equivalent range that year for the University of Puerto Rico was $790–$1,245.

The island's public institutions of higher education have implemented huge increases in spending per student over time (see figure 5-3). The result is that, despite its far lower income level, Puerto Rico spends about the same amount per student in its public universities as the mainland United States).[5] Ladd and Rivera-Batiz question whether these funds are being used productively.

Only a small proportion of students in four-year higher education institutions in Puerto Rico graduate in four years. At the University of Puerto Rico in Río Piedras, for example, only 12.5 percent of the freshman class completes its degree in four years.[6] About 50 percent of undergraduates finish within six years of entering the institution, but these graduation rates are

5. Total spending per student in public universities in Puerto Rico (including the University of Puerto Rico and other smaller specialized institutions) is not far below the U.S. average of $14,488.
6. University of Puerto Rico at Río Piedras (2005).

substantially lower than those for comprehensive public research universities in the United States. The authors argue for a renewed focus on improving quality, in both public and private sectors, if the tertiary education sector is to continue contributing to, instead of hindering, the island's growth prospects.

The authors find that the rate of return to an additional year of education in Puerto Rico has been essentially flat since 1970. This trend contrasts sharply with the rising rate of return to education in the United States—and other countries—over the same period.[7] One explanation relies on the rapidly rising supply of higher-educated labor, which may have constrained wage hikes for skilled workers. There is a demand-side explanation as well. Although private sector rates of return to education have risen in recent years, the wage premium for those with a college degree in the public sector has fallen continuously. That decline, plus the fact that in 2000 almost 40 percent of all employed workers with a college degree or more in the island were working for the government, could account for the lack of a stronger surge in the rate of return to education in Puerto Rico.

Summing Up

Ladd and Rivera-Batiz agree that Puerto Rico's past investments in education have contributed significantly to the island's economic growth. However, to sustain this progress, the island will need to focus on raising the quality of schooling and improving student achievement at all levels of the educational system. Unfortunately, enhancing quality is far more difficult than increasing quantity. Despite sharply rising funding for both K–12 and postsecondary education in recent years, the quality has not improved. Moreover, almost fifteen years of governance reforms have not produced many positive results from the schools sector, and additional governance reforms, particularly in the area of accountability, are likely to have only a small impact in the absence of other reforms. The authors suggest that Puerto Rico should focus on improving the academic environment and the quality of curriculum and instruction at the classroom level, in both K–12 and higher education. In addition, Puerto Rico faces wide gaps in schooling between socioeconomic groups. The poor have higher dropout rates and lower college entrance rates, face lower quality of schooling, and end up

7. Katz and Autor (1999); Pavcnik (2003). Note, however, that Bosworth and Collins (2006) find that the wage premium in Puerto Rico has been either flat or increasing, depending on definitions and methodology.

with little access to the highly remunerated sectors of the Puerto Rican labor market. Renewed efforts are required to diminish such inequities.

In his comments, Alan Krueger emphasized caution in interpreting the evidence of declining quality of education. It is a claim that has been repeated for generations, but the evidence is limited even in the case of Puerto Rico. There has been a very large change in the socioeconomic composition of the students: school attendance expanded to include children from low-income families, while many high-income families appear to have enrolled their children in the private system. In addition, there is a paucity of test data on which to evaluate the system's performance. Carlos Santiago agreed that the quality of the educational system was a critical issue for investigation and thought that it might be too soon to evaluate some of the educational reforms. He also pointed to the growing importance of research institutions as catalysts for economic development and wondered if such institutions were making contributions in Puerto Rico.

6

The Climate for Business Development and Employment Growth

STEVEN J. DAVIS AND LUIS A. RIVERA-BATIZ

Puerto Rico has struggled with an employment shortfall of stunning dimensions. The employment rate among working-age persons stood at nearly 50 percent in the early 1950s, then declined over the rest of the decade and again after 1971 to reach levels below 35 percent in the early 1980s. In the past thirty years, Puerto Rican employment rates range from 55 to 65 percent of U.S. rates. This huge employment shortfall holds for men and women, cuts across all education groups, and is deeper for persons without a college degree—about four-fifths of Puerto Rico's working-age population. The shortfall is concentrated in the private sector, especially in labor-intensive industries.

To help shed light on the reasons for Puerto Rico's persistently low rate of employment, Steven Davis and Luis Rivera-Batiz examine differences between Puerto Rico and the United States in the industry and size structure of employment and its division between the public and private sectors. As reported in table 6-1, only 37.5 percent of Puerto Rican residents (aged sixteen to sixty-five) held a job during the reference week of the 2000 household census, compared to 68.8 percent for the United States. The census data show similarly large employment disparities in 1980 and 1990. Data from the labor force survey present a less dire picture in more recent years,

Table 6-1. *Employment Rate, Puerto Rico and the United States, by Schooling, 1980, 1990, 2000* [a]

Percent

Schooling and year	Overall economy		Private sector		Free enterprise		Public sector	
	United States	Puerto Rico	United States	Puerto Rico	United States	Puerto Rico	United States	Puerto Rico
All levels								
1980	65.2	38.5	53.0	25.3	46.9	21.8	12.2	13.2
1990	70.0	42.3	58.4	29.1	51.1	24.9	11.6	13.2
2000	68.8	37.5	58.2	28.2	51.0	24.0	10.6	9.3
More than fourteen years								
1980	78.8	66.1	56.8	33.8	49.6	28.7	21.9	32.3
1990	84.5	70.6	64.0	39.6	55.4	33.3	20.5	31.0
2000	82.5	61.6	63.9	40.7	56.8	35.9	18.6	20.9
More than sixteen years								
1980	83.4	76.8	55.5	34.1	47.9	27.5	27.9	42.6
1990	85.5	75.2	62.7	39.8	53.6	32.6	22.8	35.4
2000	83.3	65.5	63.1	41.3	55.7	35.5	20.2	24.2

Source: Data from household census for 1980, 1990, and 2000; authors' calculations.

a. The data are for persons aged sixteen to sixty-five. The public sector includes all employees of federal and subfederal governments. The private sector encompasses the rest of the economy. The free enterprise segment of the private sector excludes nongovernmental employees in public utilities and sanitary services, primary and secondary education, colleges and universities, construction and several small industries for which public sector employment exceeds 35 percent of industry employment in Puerto Rico. For 1990 these industries are museums, galleries, and zoos; business, trade, and vocational schools; bus service and urban transit; research, development, and testing; social services; forestry; libraries. For 1980 the excluded industries are nearly identical. For 2000 the set is slightly narrower. Unpaid family workers are not counted among the employed.

but they confirm that Puerto Rico's employment rate has been remarkably low in recent decades.

The U.S.–Puerto Rican gap in private sector employment rates is even more extreme. According to census data, only 28 percent of Puerto Rican adults worked in the private sector in 2000, less than half the 58 percent figure for the mainland. A similar pattern prevailed in 1980 and 1990. These private sector employment figures overstate first-hand exposure to employment in the unfettered "free enterprise" segment of the formal economy. Indeed, many Puerto Ricans with private sector jobs work in industries with a major government role (for example, hospitals and schools), industries that owe their Puerto Rican operations to special tax subsidies (such as pharmaceuticals), or industries that face costly bureaucratic obstacles to business activity (such as construction). Similar remarks apply to many private sector jobs on the U.S. mainland, but the government's role is typically more extensive on the island.

The employment shortfall is most evident in the free enterprise segment, which comprises businesses that operate in the formal economy without large subsidies, special regulatory advantages, or heavy-handed oversight by government bureaucracies. Even by rather relaxed criteria, less than one-quarter of working-age Puerto Ricans hold a job in the free enterprise segment of the economy. By the same criteria, more than half hold free enterprise jobs on the mainland.

Low levels of work experience in free enterprise activity are potentially important for at least three reasons. First, jobs in the free enterprise segment probably require somewhat different skills and work habits than jobs in the public and regulated sectors. This view resonates with evidence that experience-related human capital is imperfectly portable across industries and evidence that many displaced workers suffer large and persistent earnings losses.[1] Thus the skills and earnings potential acquired through work experience in the public and regulated sectors may not easily transfer to free enterprise work activity.

Second, private sector work experience is a more powerful incubator of entrepreneurial skills and ambitions than jobs in the public and regulated sectors. This proposition finds support in previous research on the propensity to become a business owner and the determinants of business success. Studies consistently find that self-employment and business ownership rates are much higher among children of business owners.[2] Based on U.S. data, Fairlie and Robb report that half of all business owners had a self-employed family member before starting a business.[3]

Third, the nature of work experience, one's own and that of friends and family, probably plays an important role in shaping attitudes toward business regulation, taxation, public sector employment, and income redistribution. There is a greater belief in the propositions that "poverty is society's fault" and "luck determines income" in countries with higher social welfare spending.[4] And there is stronger support for the view that "it is the responsibility of the government to reduce income differences" in countries with a history of socialized production.[5] These cross-country patterns suggest

1. See Neal (1995); Parent (2000); Jacobson, LaLonde, and Sullivan (1993).
2. Recent studies on this issue include Dunn and Holtz-Eakin (2000); Hout and Rosen (2000); and Fairlie and Robb (2003).
3. Fairlie and Robb (2003).
4. See Alesina and Glaeser (2004, chap. 7).
5. Corneo and Gruener (2002, table 1).

Table 6-2. *College-Educated Workers in the Private Sector and the Free Enterprise Segment as Share of Working-Age Persons, Puerto Rico and the United States, 1980, 1990, 2000* [a]

Percent

	Private sector employment			Free enterprise segment employment		
Year	Puerto Rico	United States	United States/ Puerto Rico	Puerto Rico	United States	United States/ Puerto Rico
1980	2.9	8.1	2.8	2.3	7.0	3.0
1990	5.2	10.1	1.9	4.3	8.7	2.0
2000	6.9	14.2	2.1	5.9	12.6	2.1

Source: Data from household census for 1980, 1990, and 2000; authors' calculations.

a. The data are for persons aged sixteen to sixty-five. The private sector encompasses all workers except employees of federal and subfederal governments. The free enterprise segment of the private sector excludes nongovernmental employees in public utilities and sanitary services, primary and secondary education, colleges and universities, construction and several small industries for which public sector employment exceeds 35 percent of industry employment in Puerto Rico. For 1990 these industries are museums, galleries, and zoos; business, trade, and vocational schools; bus service and urban transit; research, development, and testing; social services; forestry; libraries. For 1980 the excluded industries are nearly identical. For 2000 the set is slightly narrower. Unpaid family workers are not counted among the employed.

that limited work experience in free enterprise activity limits political support for economic reforms that would expand private business activity and employment.

The strikingly underdeveloped state of the Puerto Rican private sector supports the view that Puerto Rico suffers from an inhospitable business climate. Looking at employment rates by sector and educational attainment, Davis and Rivera-Batiz also found significant gaps between the United States and Puerto Rico. Table 6-2 combines data on the population's schooling distribution and employment rates by schooling levels to calculate the percentage of adults who are college educated and working in the private sector. Relative to the population, college-educated persons working in the private sector were nearly three times more abundant on the mainland than on the island in 1980, and roughly twice as abundant in 1990 and 2000. A similar pattern holds with respect to college-educated persons working in the free enterprise segment of the economy. Davis and Rivera-Batiz designate the same set of industries as constituting the free enterprise segment in Puerto Rico and the United States, even though the government role at the industry level looms larger in Puerto Rico. For this reason, the authors think the results in table 6-2 understate the relative scarcity of college-educated Puerto Ricans engaged in free enterprise work activity.

Further analysis demonstrates that Puerto Rico's industry structure has, for decades, been grossly misaligned with the human capital mix of its population. As evidence of this misalignment, the authors consider the relationship between the schooling intensity of the industry employment distribution and the schooling attainment of the working-age population. They calculate a state-level measure of schooling intensity in two steps. In the first step, they compute the schooling intensity of each census industry as the mean years of completed schooling among all U.S. workers in the industry, weighting each worker in proportion to hours worked. In the second step, they calculate a schooling intensity index for each state (and for the commonwealth) as the employment-weighted mean of the industry-level schooling intensity values. By construction, an industry has the same schooling intensity in all states and in Puerto Rico. So, the index quantifies the extent to which the employment distribution tilts toward schooling-intensive industries.

Figure 6-1 demonstrates that mean years of schooling among Puerto Rican adults fell well short of that in any U.S. state in 2000. Nevertheless, the schooling intensity of Puerto Rico's industry mix exceeds that of two-thirds of the fifty states. In terms of schooling intensity, Puerto Rico's industry mix ranked sixteenth out of fifty-one in 2000 (tied with Utah and Washington). The same pattern held in 1980 and 1990, even though the schooling attainment of Puerto Ricans lagged even further behind the mainland in these earlier years. Thus the Puerto Rican economy has for decades failed to generate jobs that matched the educational qualifications of the Puerto Rican population.

Put differently, the missing jobs in Puerto Rico are concentrated in labor-intensive industries that rely heavily on less-educated workers. For example, Puerto Rico's employment rate in Eating, Drinking, and Lodging is lower than the rate for *any* state in recent decades and less than one-third the rate in Hawaii. The persistent inability of the Puerto Rican economy to generate jobs that match the human capital mix of its population testifies to a profound failure of industrial and employment policy.

The evidence does not support the view that more schooling can, by itself, resolve Puerto Rico's employment problems. Very large gains in schooling attainment in recent decades have accompanied very modest employment gains. To provide additional insight into the nature of Puerto Rico's employment shortfall, the authors also relate the industry structure of employment to the schooling attainment of employed persons rather than all working-age persons. As seen in figure 6-2, Puerto Rico remains an outlier in 2000 in this respect, but no more so than Texas, California, or New Mexico. In other words, Puerto Rico achieved a reasonable alignment between its industry structure and the educational

Figure 6-1. *Schooling Intensity of State's Industry Mix, by Mean Schooling Years of Its Adult Population, 2000*[a]

Schooling intensity

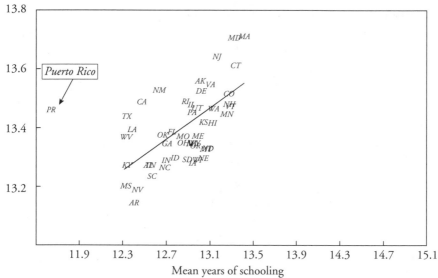

Mean years of schooling

Source: Data from Ruggles and others (2004); authors' calculations.

a. Mean schooling years is calculated as the simple mean years of completed schooling among residents sixteen to sixty-five years old. For education codes not specified in terms of years of schooling, we assigned approximate values. For example, "associate degree" in 1990 and 2000 became fourteen years of schooling. The schooling intensity of the states' industry employment mix is an index constructed in two steps. First, the schooling intensity of each census industry was computed as the hours-weighted mean years of completed schooling among all U.S. workers in the industry. Industry affiliation reflects the worker's current primary job, defined as the one that generates the largest earnings. The hours-worked measure pertains to the reference week in the 1980 and 1990 census and to usual hours worked each week during the previous calendar year in the 2000 census. Second, the schooling intensity index for the state or commonwealth industry distribution was computed as the employment-weighted mean of the industry-level schooling intensity values. By construction, an industry has the same schooling intensity in all states and in Puerto Rico. The index quantifies the extent to which a state's industry mix tilts toward schooling-intensive industries, as measured by the industry workforce in the United States.

attainment of employed persons by 2000—roughly in line with the relationship among the fifty states—but it did so by excluding the less educated from jobs.

Relative to the United States, Puerto Rico's employment shortfall exceeds 10 percent of the population for college-educated persons and 20 percent or more for groups with less education. Thus, if and when Puerto Rico matches U.S. schooling levels, very large employment shortfalls will persist in the absence of deep reforms.

Davis and Rivera-Batiz point out that no single policy or institutional deficiency fully accounts for Puerto Rico's huge employment shortfall,

Figure 6-2. *Schooling Intensity of State's Industry Mix, by Mean Schooling Years of Its Workers, 2000*[a]

Schooling intensity

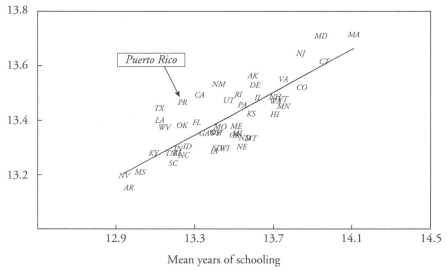

Mean years of schooling

Source: Data from Ruggles and others (2004), authors' calculations.

a. Mean schooling years were calculated as the simple mean years of completed schooling among employed persons sixteen to sixty-five years old. In other respects, the calculations follow those used in figure 6-1. Note that the range of the horizontal axes is 2.0 years in figure 6-2 but 3.6 years in figure 6-1.

underdeveloped private sector, and misaligned industry structure. Indeed, their analysis yields a long and varied list of significant contributing factors:

—Large government transfer payments undermine work incentives and contribute to a deficit of work experience and marketable skills.

—Minimum wage laws discourage the hiring of less skilled workers, suppress the growth of employment in industries and activities that rely heavily on less educated workers, and diminish opportunities to acquire experience and training on the job.

—Historically, the large role for public sector employment and production in Puerto Rico has softened competitive pressures on the island and discouraged the emergence of a vibrant private sector.

—Section 936 of the U.S. tax code and other federal tax incentives have helped create an industry structure in Puerto Rico that is poorly aligned with the type of job opportunities needed by its population. At best, section 936 provided for a modest number of jobs in Puerto Rico at enormous cost to the U.S. Treasury.

—Puerto Rico's own tax code is replete with provisions that benefit special business interests at the expense of the general welfare. These tax code provisions both reflect and contribute to a business climate in which profitability and survival too often rest on the ability to obtain favors from the government, rather than the ability to innovate, raise productivity, and serve consumers.

—Puerto Rico's regulatory environment deters business entry, hampers job creation, and erodes competitive pressures in many ways. Occupational licensing requirements create artificial entry barriers, restricting the supply of services and raising prices to consumers. Government oversight of business entry and location decisions raises entry costs and affords commercial rivals the opportunity to block entry. "Buy local" laws insulate business interests from foreign competition and raise prices for consumers. Like many provisions of the tax code, these aspects of the regulatory environment serve special business interests at the expense of the general welfare. They reflect and promote a business culture focused on rent seeking.

—The permitting process—whereby the government oversees construction and real estate development projects, the commercial use of equipment and facilities, and the periodic renewal of various business licenses—suffers from several serious problems. These problems raise the costs of doing business, undercut the drive for employment growth, and retard economic development.

As part of their study, the authors interviewed more than one hundred persons who have expertise or first-hand experience with the permitting process. Most shared the view that the permitting process is excessively slow and costly, fraught with uncertainty and unpredictability, prone to corruption, and susceptible to manipulation by business rivals, politicians, and special interest groups. Independent evidence from public sources supports these claims.

Efforts to reform the permitting process have met with very limited success. A partial exception is the Autonomous Municipalities Law of 1991, which allows municipal governments to take over much of the permitting process from the governor's office if the municipality meets several conditions. Many interviewees stated that the permitting process functions much more smoothly in a handful of autonomous municipalities. However, the approach provided by the Autonomous Municipalities Law offers at best a partial solution to problems in the permitting process. Fourteen years after the law's enactment, only six municipalities had achieved autonomous status. For reasons of insufficient scale, limited financial resources, and lack of personnel, it is doubtful whether the other seventy-two municipalities can efficiently manage the permitting process, at least in its current form.

The study emphasizes employment outcomes, but the policies and institutional arrangements discussed by the authors also lower real incomes and living standards by undermining productivity. Transfer payments and minimum wage laws lower worker productivity by contributing to a deficit of work experience. Special-interest tax subsidies distort market price signals that would otherwise guide capital and labor to their best uses, lowering productivity in the process. Inefficiencies in the permitting process raise the cost of doing business, lowering productivity directly. Regulatory entry barriers, "buy local" laws, and a large role for the public sector soften competitive pressures on the island. In turn, softer competition weakens the pressure to innovate and provide value for customers. Artificial entry barriers and inefficiencies in the permitting process also retard the type of creative destruction process that transformed the U.S. retail sector in recent decades, bringing dramatic productivity gains for businesses and lower prices and wider product selections for consumers. Finally, institutional arrangements that foster rent-seeking behavior lower productivity because they encourage socially wasteful efforts to curry favor with government officials and secure preferential treatment, rather than socially productive efforts to better serve customers, improve products, and expand markets.

In her comments, Marinés Aponte argued that the authors take too narrow a view of the determinants of entrepreneurial opportunities by focusing on government policies and the permitting process. She emphasized that assistance to business start-ups is extensive in Puerto Rico. She also said that the tax preferences provided to U.S. firms operating in Puerto Rico had created an unequal playing field that may make it hard for local firms to compete. David Audretsch agreed that there is a need to reduce barriers to business start-ups. He also pointed to the inability of some countries to translate large investments in education and R&D into rapid growth. He suggested that new businesses might be an important mechanism for translating new knowledge into commercial development.

7

Assessing Puerto Rico's Fiscal Policies

JAMES ALM

Puerto Rico's fiscal system has undergone major changes in recent years. While these changes have been beneficial in various dimensions, the system remains plagued by problems. Alm provides a critical assessment, addressing the role of fiscal deficits and some features of public expenditure. He focuses on the tax side, emphasizing extensive tax evasion with a shrinking tax base, weak tax administration, an unnecessarily complex tax system, and overuse of tax incentives. These features interact to undermine government effectiveness in promoting development and economic growth.

Beyond the limitations of the tax system, there are other persistent and growing fiscal problems. Table 7-1 shows that revenues have been insufficient to cover current expenditures. Thus, in most years over the past two decades, fiscal deficits have been the usual outcome.

Short- and long-term public debt has been growing more rapidly than either gross national product (GNP) or gross domestic product (GDP). The budget for fiscal year 2004–05 was enacted with a deficit forecast at $550 million, and accumulated government debt is now roughly $13 billion. To camouflage the magnitude of the deficit, the government has increased its reliance on nonrecurring revenues. Although major new infrastructure projects (for example, an urban train, a coliseum, and a transshipping port) have

Table 7-1. *General Government Expenditures and Revenue in Puerto Rico,*
1990–2004
Thousands of U.S.$

	1990	1995	2000	2001	2002	2003	2004
Revenues	6,465	8,082	10,855	11,208	11,659	12,183	12,100
Outlays	6,807	8,121	11,283	12,008	13,031	13,785	14,445
Overall balance (change in cash minus net debt issues)	−342	−39	−429	−800	−1,372	−1,602	−2,345

Source: Puerto Rico Department of Treasury, *Comprehensive Annual Financial Report,* annual publications for 1990–2004; Statement of Revenue, Expenditures, and Changes in Fund Balances, Total Governmental Funds.

been finished or will be completed in the near future, no funds have been allocated to finance their operations. Numerous government enterprises that operate largely as separate units remain the financial responsibility of the government. Furthermore, the pension fund for public employees has unfunded liabilities amounting to more than $11 billion. If nothing is done, this actuarial deficit implies future payments out of tax revenues, with concomitant higher fiscal deficits in the future.

As a result of these and other factors, credit rating agencies have recently downgraded the government's bond rating. Indeed, in May 2005 this rating was lowered to the bottom of the investment grade category (BBB and Baa2), reflecting the use of nonrecurring revenues to finance the operating fund deficit, as well as the looming shortfalls in the pension fund. More broadly, the quality of public expenditures in such basic areas as education, public infrastructure, and security is perceived as so lacking that many individuals and businesses have resorted to making their own private expenditures to ensure adequate services.

The Puerto Rican Tax System

The current tax system in Puerto Rico was structured at the beginning of the 1950s as part of a broader attempt to industrialize and modernize the economy. The policies enacted at that time reflected conventional wisdom about development strategies in the immediate postwar era: state provision of incentives through tax exemptions and of direct subsidies to firms promoted by the Administracion de Fomento Económico (the Puerto Rican Industrial Development Company), and state participation in constructing the infrastructure for modernization. Although the tax system has been reformed on several occasions since then (in 1975, 1987, and 1994), the legacy of the 1950s remains strong.[1]

Taxes (direct and indirect) are the main source of revenue for the General Fund. Direct taxes, derived mainly from taxing the income of persons and firms, contributed over three-fourths of the tax revenue of the General Fund in 2002. *Arbitrios* (excise taxes) are the other important category of funds, constituting 22.8 percent of the tax revenue in the General Fund in 2002. There is also a tax on inheritance and donations, but revenues from this source are quite small, only 0.1 percent of the total tax revenues. Property taxes are also an unimportant source of revenues, largely because the tax base is greatly undervalued (assessments are based on the value that would have existed in 1958), even though the statutory tax rates (which vary marginally across municipalities) fluctuate around 8 percent.

Tax revenue relative to GDP increased from 12.1 percent in 1950 to 15.1 percent in 1990. At the beginning of the 1950s a tax restructuring made possible a significant increase in the collection of taxes as a percentage of GDP. In the second half of the 1970s there was another increase in the share of the tax collections, after the reform of 1975 (which introduced new taxes and increased the tax rates) and the adoption in 1976 of the Internal Revenue Code of the United States.

Benchmarking the Puerto Rican Tax System

The author then compares the practice of taxation and expenditures in Puerto Rico to international practice, along several dimensions. As shown in table 7-2, two of the main features that emerge from the analysis are that Puerto Rico generates considerably more revenue from its corporate income tax (as a percentage of total revenues) than the "typical" U.S. state and local government, and considerably less revenue from its collection of excise taxes than the average U.S. subnational government.

Taxes as a percentage of gross income are significantly higher in Puerto Rico than in the typical U.S. state. However, the per capita level of Puerto Rican taxes is somewhat lower than the average state and local government sector in the United States. Furthermore, as shown in table 7-3, the composition of expenditures in Puerto Rico is roughly the same as that in the average U.S. state, although Puerto Rico spends slightly more heavily on health and less heavily on education than the average mainland state.

1. Cao García (2004).

Table 7-2. *Distribution of Taxes and Total Taxes for Puerto Rico and Selected States, 2002*

Percent of total taxes unless otherwise indicated

Puerto Rico or state	Individual income	Corporate income	Sales and gross receipts	Property	Motor vehicle	Other	Total taxes (percent of gross income)[a]	Total taxes per capita (U.S.$)
Puerto Rico	39.3	36.6	22.8	. . .	0.01	1.3	14.3	1,669.9
U.S. state and local total	22.4	3.1	35.8	30.8	1.9	5.95	8.6	3,140.5
Alabama	21.9	3.3	49.4	15.2	2.1	5.9	7.7	2,169.9
Louisiana	14.7	2.2	57.0	15.9	1.0	5.9	9.3	2,721.6
Mississippi	15.1	3.0	49.9	25.2	1.7	2.1	9.4	2,275.5
New Jersey	19.8	3.2	25.4	46.4	1.1	2.5	9.1	4,038.3

Source: Planning Board of Puerto Rico, *Economic Report to the Governor, 2004 Statistical Appendix;* U.S. Census Bureau, *State and Local Government Finances.*

a. For U.S. states, as percent of gross state product. For Puerto Rico, as a percent of gross income.

Table 7-3. *Distribution of Current Expenditure Categories for Puerto Rico and Selected States, 2003*
Percent of current expenditure

Puerto Rico or state	Education	Public safety	Health	Housing and welfare	Other[a]
Puerto Rico	28.0	12.1	16.2	25.1	18.7
U.S. state average	37.4	12.6	10.0	23.0	16.9
Alabama	40.2	7.1	18.5	25.0	9.2
Louisiana	41.8	10.5	16.1	16.8	14.8
Mississippi	39.1	6.3	13.7	30.0	10.9
New Jersey	45.7	10.6	6.2	18.5	19.0

Source: Puerto Rico Department of Treasury, *Comprehensive Annual Financial Report 2004;* U.S. Census Bureau, *State and Local Government Finances.*

a. For Puerto Rico, "Other" includes general government and economic development. For U.S. states, "Other" includes general government, transportation, and natural resources.

Alm then compares the Puerto Rican system of taxation with that of other countries, especially smaller countries and those in the Caribbean. Comparing the level of taxation in Puerto Rico (as a percentage of GDP in 2001) with taxation in a group of "small" Caribbean and Central American countries for which data are available, he found that taxes relative to GDP are somewhat lower for Puerto Rico (23.3 percent) than for the median of other small countries (29.1 percent). However, Puerto Rican taxes are quite high relative to income (36.4 percent).

Using IMF data, Alm also compared the tax ratio (tax as a share of GDP) for 117 countries. The average for this sample of countries in 2001 was 23.6 percent of GDP, nearly identical to the ratio for Puerto Rico. This simple comparison suggests that Puerto Rico has about an average level of taxation. However, averages are misleading because countries have very different capacities to tax.

On the basis of this international comparison, Alm concludes that Puerto Rico's taxes relative to GDP are average, neither high nor low. Some could point to this tax rate as one of the competitive features of the Puerto Rican economy and argue that taxes should be held at their present level. Others may see this feature as evidence that there is at least some room for additional taxes.

The author then analyzes whether Puerto Rico's tax *structure* (as opposed to tax *level*) is similar to that of other countries. This analysis demonstrates that the burden of income taxation (measured by income taxes as a percentage of total taxes, where income taxes include individual, corporate, and payroll taxes, where relevant) is considerably higher, and that of sales taxes is considerably lower, for Puerto Rico than for most of the countries included in the sample. These tax structure differences suggest that income taxes, particularly individual income taxes, are used much more heavily in Puerto Rico than in most other countries and that Puerto Rico taxes labor heavily. It would take a significant reduction in income taxes to bring Puerto Rico to a level of direct tax reliance similar to that observed elsewhere. The data also suggest that Puerto Rico taxes consumption much less heavily than most countries do.

Analyzing the personal income tax by itself, Alm finds that Puerto Rico generates roughly the average amount of revenue from the personal income tax, relative to selected countries of roughly similar size. Nevertheless, the combined importance of individual and corporate income taxes in total taxes is considerably higher in Puerto Rico than in many countries.

By comparing actual income tax revenue with estimated potential income tax revenue, Alm calculates indexes of tax effort for the countries in the sample, and he then uses regression results to estimate an expected or predicted level of individual income tax for Puerto Rico. For the 1990–2000 period, Alm predicts that a country of Puerto Rico's income, population, and openness would raise 3.3 percent of its GDP in individual income tax revenue. In fact, Puerto Rico raises 5.2 percent, well above the predicted amount. Puerto Rico's tax effort index for the individual income tax (or the actual percentage of individual income tax revenue divided by the estimated percentage) is 1.58, among the largest in the sample. This analysis shows that Puerto Rico has a relatively large yield from the individual income tax. These international comparisons suggest that there is not much room for increasing the effective tax rate for the individual income tax.

Evaluating the Puerto Rico Tax System

Tax systems are designed to achieve multiple objectives. One obvious purpose is to raise the revenues necessary to finance government expenditures; another is to ensure that the growth in revenues is adequate to meet expenditure requirements. Yet another is to distribute the burden of taxation in a way that meets with a society's notions of fairness; such "equity" is typically defined in terms of "ability to pay," such that those with equal ability should pay equal taxes and those with greater ability should pay greater taxes. Taxes can also be used to influence the behavior of those who pay them; in choosing taxes, a common goal of policymakers is to minimize the interference of taxes in the economic decisions of individuals and firms. Taxes should be simple, both to administer and to comply with, because a complicated tax system wastes the resources of tax administrators and taxpayers.

Alm analyzes the performance of the Puerto Rican tax system and reaches the following conclusions. First, by all accounts, large amounts of income and consumption escape taxation in Puerto Rico. Some analysts estimate that uncollected personal income taxes amounted to 29.7 percent of actual income tax revenues in 1987 and 24.9 percent of tax revenues in 1992.[2] Estimates of the size of the underground economy in Puerto Rico are also quite large.[3]

Second, Alm discusses Puerto Rico's tax base. The goal of most tax reforms is to broaden the base, thereby allowing marginal tax rates to be reduced. However, the tax base in Puerto Rico has been narrowed in at least two important ways. One is legal, taking the form of exemptions or preferential treatment (such as "tax expenditures"). There is no systematic listing of the tax expenditures in the Puerto Rican tax system, a problem in itself. The other stems from administrative failures (especially enforcement problems) that allow tax evasion on a large scale. One result of a small and shrinking tax base is that the government must emphasize collection of taxes from those "tax handles" that are readily available. The more visible taxpayers (such as wage earners) end up bearing disproportionate amounts of the tax burden.

Third, Alm stresses the excessive use of tax incentives, particularly in the corporate income tax, which has been central to Puerto Rican development policy over the past fifty years. It is frequently argued that, without fiscal incentives, Puerto Rican firms (especially those in manufacturing and tourism) simply could not compete in the world economy. However, the author points out that evaluations of benefits and costs are seldom done.

After one such evaluation, however, Indonesia eliminated all of its investment incentives as part of a comprehensive tax reform in the mid-1980s.[4] There was much evidence that few if any incentives had produced the desired effects, accomplishing instead only a massive loss in tax revenues. Further, although tax incentives may have attracted investment, they were not on balance beneficial to the Indonesian economy. Tax incentives were also associated with enormous administrative problems, especially for tax holidays. The presence of tax incentives for some groups of taxpayers

---

2. Toledo and Camacho (1997).
3. See Schneider and Enste (2002) and Bosworth and Collins (2006, appendix 2B).
4. See Gillis (1985).

required higher tax rates on other nonfavored taxpayers, and these taxpayers lobbied for their own special treatment. Finally, smaller firms had been an important source of job growth in Indonesia but did not usually receive tax incentives. On balance, the costs were deemed to be far in excess of the potential benefits. In particular, there was little evidence that the incentives were more important to potential investors than such factors as political stability, potential market size, economic growth, or infrastructure. As a result, the best policy for investment in Indonesia was deemed to be a reduction in the corporate income tax rate.

Indeed, there is now some broader evidence that the best way to encourage investment is simply to lower the corporate income tax rate, not to offer targeted incentives. There is also increasing evidence that the main effect of tax incentives is on the transfer of income across jurisdictions (via such mechanisms as transfer pricing and financial policies) rather than on the location of real activity across jurisdictions.[5] The main messages of this research are that tax incentives can stimulate investment, but that a country's overall economic characteristics are much more important for the success or failure of industries than any tax incentive package. Even if tax incentives stimulate investment, they are not usually cost-effective.

Closely related to the issue of tax incentives is the notion that the tax system can be used to encourage economic growth. Alm notes that a large literature attempts to demonstrate this link. Much of this literature focuses on the experience of U.S. states and examines whether there is a connection between state tax policies and economic growth. Recent work on the effects of measurement error and estimation technique finds some connections between policy variables and economic growth, but these results are not very robust.[6] For example, higher state tax revenues are associated with lower growth rates in some specifications. Other research has found weak evidence that the mix of taxes (for example, a heavier reliance on income taxes or sales taxes) affects state economic growth. As for state expenditure policy, some analysts find that higher welfare expenditures are correlated with lower economic growth, as expected, but greater spending on education and highways tends to be negatively associated with state economic growth. In short, there is some connection between policy variables and economic growth, but the connection is tenuous and is not robust across all time periods, estimation methods, or specifications.

The author concludes that there are likely to be large efficiency costs associated with Puerto Rican taxes. A commonly accepted notion about "good"

5. See Grubert and Slemrod (1998).
6. See Alm and Rogers (2005).

tax policy is that the tax system should raise revenues with minimal interference in the decisions of consumers and firms. When a tax leads individuals and businesses to change their decisions, then the tax is said to impose an efficiency cost, or an "excess burden." The system of taxes in Puerto Rico, particularly the corporate income tax, is likely to introduce a wide range of distortions in individual and firm behavior. Together with the extensive system of tax incentives, the corporate tax gives preferential treatment both to different types of investment and to different sectors, leading firms to base their investment decisions mainly on tax considerations rather than on market forces. According to Alm, this use of tax incentives to increase investment and to generate growth is a questionable and unproven practice. The personal income tax also generates distortions by discouraging work effort, reducing the return to savings, encouraging the overuse of items that are tax deductible or that generate tax credits, and encouraging individuals to move to the informal sector. Unfortunately, there are no estimates of the overall efficiency cost of Puerto Rican taxes.

Public Debt in Puerto Rico

Public debt complements taxes and federal transfers in financing government expenditures. When public debt is issued, the funds are available and used in the present, but the obligation to repay the debt is in the future. Through the issue of public debt, the current generation imposes a burden on future generations; the opposite occurs when public investments are financed by current fiscal income.

In Puerto Rico, over the fiscal years 1990 to 2004, GNP grew at an annual average rate of 6.4 percent, while total public debt grew at an annual rate of 7.4 percent. Figure 7-1 shows the evolution of public debt of state enterprises, debt issued by the central government, and municipal debt over 1989–2004. These grew at average annual rates of 7.2, 7.3, and 11.5 percent, respectively.

The more rapid growth of public debt than of GNP has contributed to the continual downgrading of the government's bond rating. Even so, other circumstances may be of more concern. Recent budgets have been characterized by large and growing deficits, and the deficit for 2004–05 is roughly $3 billion. In the year 2003 the central government issued $2 billion in long-term debt to refinance short-term loans previously issued by the Government Development Bank to finance past budget deficits. State enterprises regularly capitalize maintenance expenditures and finance them through long-term public debt. Legislators use "pork barrel" funds for social expenditures (such

Figure 7-1. *Public Debt in Puerto Rico, 1989–2004*
Millions of dollars

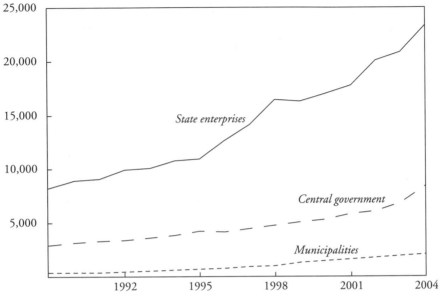

Source: Data from Puerto Rico Planning Board, *Economic Report to the Governor, Statistical Appendix,* various years.

as current outlays) but they are financed out of public debt. There are major unfunded infrastructure projects that are the responsibility of the government. A sizable portion of the debt is regularly used to finance current expenditures, instead of public investment; future generations receive no benefits from these current expenditures, but they will have the burden of paying the debt and the accrued interest, leaving a smaller proportion of future current revenues to finance discretionary expenses in the government budget. The pension fund for public employees has enormous—and growing—unfunded liabilities. In the three years 2001–04, pension contributions averaged only about half of the annual pension cost, and the unfunded liabilities of the pension system amounted to more than $11 billion at the end of 2004. Overall, there is little doubt that there are major structural imbalances in the budget situation of the Puerto Rican government.

Public Expenditures in Puerto Rico

Public expenditures exhibited an upward trend from 1955 to 1975, increasing from 12.2 percent of GNP in 1955 to 22.5 percent in 1975, while invest-

Figure 7-2. *Revenues and Outlays as a Percentage of GNP, 1990–2004*

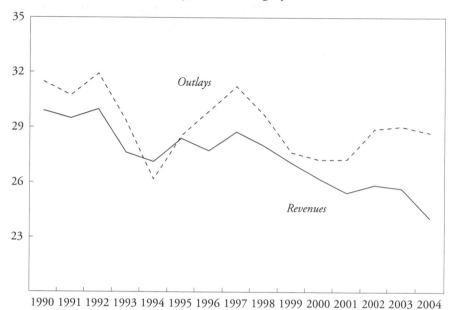

Source: Puerto Rico Department of Treasury, *Comprehensive Annual Financial Report,* annual publications for 1990–2004; Statement of Revenue, Expenditures, and Changes in Fund Balances, Total Governmental Funds.

ment expenditures increased from 2.4 percent of GNP in 1955 to 3.9 percent in 1975. A fiscal crisis in 1975 resulted in the shrinking of the relative size of the government until 1982. This was followed by a period of sustained, albeit slow, growth in the relative share of government until 1997, when combined expenditures (consumption and investment) reached 25 percent of GNP. As shown in figure 7-2, the relative size of government fell from 1997 to 2000, and the next four years showed oscillations, with no definite pattern.

The relative size of the central government today is smaller than it was thirty years ago. Indeed, it should also be noted that central government outlays as a percentage of GNP in Puerto Rico tend to be lower than in most developed countries. The common notion that the government has grown "too big" in Puerto Rico cannot easily be justified by the actual relative size of central government expenditures in economic activity.

To expand the analysis, Alm considers the "consolidated budget," or the central government plus state enterprise outlays. Consolidated budget outlays as a percentage of GNP were in the range of 50 to 57 percent between fiscal years 1977 and 1987. In 1988 the consolidated budget rose suddenly and peaked at 61 percent of GNP in 1990; thereafter the percentage returned to 50–55 percent and stayed within this range until 1999. In fiscal year 1999 there was a sharp decline in the relative size of outlays because of the privatization of the telephone company, and in the year 2000 the size of government fell to its minimum value of 44 percent of GNP for the period under consideration. Since then, the share of government has shown a slight upward trend, reaching 47 percent in fiscal year 2004.

Even when state enterprises are included, the relative size of government today is smaller than it was thirty years ago. Any discontent with government in public opinion therefore is likely about something other than the size of outlays.

Reforming the Puerto Rican Fiscal System

The current fiscal system of Puerto Rico has some significant strengths. Nonetheless, improvements can still be made. The author suggests five reforms. First is to change the tax structure, while not increasing tax effort. Second is to change the composition of taxation toward more reliance on indirect taxation. Third, Alm calls for simplifying the tax system, especially in the use of tax incentives. Fourth is to expand the bases of the various taxes (especially individual and corporate income taxes), thereby reducing the burden on wage earners in the formal sector, allowing reductions in the marginal tax rates, and reducing the distortions now present in the tax system. Finally, Alm calls for improving tax administration in order to reduce tax evasion.

This chapter's three discussants, Ronald Fisher, William Lockwood Benet, and Fuat Andic, raised concerns related to Puerto Rico's fiscal difficulties that they believe warrant additional attention. All three emphasized the expenditure side of the budget. Andic stressed that expenditure reforms must be addressed first. Fisher suggested that the growing fiscal deficit may reflect a lack of local support for public spending, which then contributed to development of a tax structure with an eroding base. Andic and especially Lockwood also stressed that fiscal policy and reform attempts on the island should increase institutional expertise and autonomy.

Both Andic and Fisher emphasized the importance of property tax reform. In this context, Fisher took issue with the characterization of the property tax in the chapter. In his view, the current version of the tax has evolved into a lump sum tax, and the proposed reforms to base the tax on property values should be analyzed as the adoption of a new tax, the expected effects of which would include a decline in the returns to investment and in Puerto Rican land values.

The discussants also stressed the need for fiscal restructuring to be more explicitly based on developments and features specific to Puerto Rico. Lockwood called for closer attention to the fiscal implications of eliminating section 936 of the 1976 Tax Reform Act. Fisher cautioned against simply following broad prescriptions, or making recommendations based on "typical" policy in comparator states or nations. Instead, he advocated tax reforms based on Puerto Rico's particular economic structure. For example, the substantial number of part-time residents may suggest an important role for consumption taxes and user fees similar to those in Florida. Fisher also gave examples to illustrate that some of the comparisons with states and countries given in the chapter may be misleading because of Puerto Rico's unusual political and fiscal features. Andic argued that a general retail sales tax, with a municipal sharing clause, would be easier to administer than a value-added tax.

8

Financing Economic Development

RITA MALDONADO-BEAR AND INGO WALTER

The financial architecture of national economies plays a critical role in economic development because it stands at the center of the capital allocation process. In this chapter, Maldonado-Bear and Walter posit a set of benchmarks for the appropriate financial architecture in the context of economic development and relate this architecture and its benchmarks to the unique context of Puerto Rico. They also develop an extensive data appendix, including balance sheet information for each segment of the financial system (see Maldonado-Bear and Walter, 2006).

The financial sector, in Puerto Rico as elsewhere, is the equivalent of a major industry in terms of output, income, growth, and tax revenue generation. A healthy, innovative, and competitively vibrant financial services sector is as essential to Puerto Rico's economic development as any other major industry, quite apart from its special role in financial intermediation, payments, and risk management. Therefore, the authors also discuss some unique dimensions of the Puerto Rican financial sector. For example, in the absence of its own currency and central bank, Puerto Rican financial institutions do not perform some of the usual foreign exchange functions. Second, as part of the U.S. payments system (the Clearing House Interbank Payments System, or CHIPS), Puerto Rico does not have to maintain the domestic payments infrastructure of a stand-alone financial system. Third, in addition to its own regulatory systems, key financial operations such as commercial banking and securities are subject as well to supervision by U.S. regulatory bodies such as the Federal Reserve and the Securities and Exchange Commission.

Maldonado-Bear and Walter then focus specifically on the contribution of the financial sector in Puerto Rico to the economic development of the island. After examining the process of intermediation on the island in its various forms, they discuss the development and present operations of the Puerto Rican financial sector.

Distribution of Assets among Financial Institutions in Puerto Rico

The authors find that total assets in the Puerto Rican financial sector were approximately $200 billion in 2004. As shown in table 8-1, these assets were distributed as follows: the banking sector held 47 percent (43 percent held by fourteen private sector commercial banks and 4 percent held by the two government banks); international banking entities (IBEs) held 30 percent; insurance companies held 6 percent; investment companies (mutual funds) held 5 percent; mortgage companies held 4 percent; credit unions held 3 percent; finance companies held 2 percent; broker-dealers held 1 percent; leasing and small loan companies held less than 1 percent each. Venture capital companies represent a tiny percent of the total financial system and are excluded from the table.

The authors carefully examine each of these financial intermediaries in terms of its present structure and function, with emphasis on both strengths and weaknesses relative to its role in the economic development of Puerto Rico. The sources and uses of funds and the profitability and efficiency of each group of financial intermediaries in the island are captured from the analysis of ten years of financial statements, which are included in the chapter.

Commercial Banks

A significant amount of data is presented in the form of text, figures, and tables relating to the current composition of the fourteen operating commercial banks in Puerto Rico, including their largest asset categories: securities holdings and real estate loans. While the growth of assets is clearly positive, the authors highlight the troubling fact that the commercial and industrial loans (C&I) segment performed below the average growth rate of assets

Table 8-1. *Financial Sector Assets as Share of Total Financial Sector Assets, Puerto Rico, Selected Years, 1995–2004*[a]

Percent, except as indicated

Institution type	1995	2000	2004	CAGR[b]
Small-loan companies	2.7	1.6	0.6	−5.5
Leasing companies	1.3	0.9	1.0	8.7
Broker-dealers	4.7	3.6	1.1	−4.6
Finance companies	2.3	3.3	2.2	11.4
Credit unions	4.1	3.2	2.8	7.6
Mortgage companies	1.6	3.3	3.8	23.2
Investment companies	0.6	1.7	5.4	43.7
Insurance companies	9.0	8.1	5.5	6.1
International banking entities	23.5	31.1	30.6	15.4
Banking sector	50.3	43.3	47.1	11.2
Total financial sector	100	100	100	12.0
Total financial sector (billions of dollars)	78	143	218	. . .

Source: Data from the Offices of the Commissioner of Financial Institutions and the Commissioner of Insurance of Puerto Rico.

a. Assets of insurance companies and credit unions were estimated as of June 2004, as the data were not available.

b. Cumulative annual growth rate, 1995–2004.

overall, while loans to individuals grew a mere 1 percent (see table 8-2). Maldonado-Bear and Walter point out that C&I lending represents precisely the type of financial intermediation that creates the greatest traction in the process of economic development, and that the commercial banks have allocated their funds to investments in securities and real estate at the expense of C&I and loans. Puerto Rico's tax structure, as it applies to banks, might be an important factor in such asset allocations.

Without discounting the many positive accomplishments of Puerto Rican banks that are set forth in the chapter, the authors also note that the sector exhibits an arguably weak balance sheet position. For example, they stress that preferred stock grew dramatically during the decade. Although still small in monetary value, it amounted to 7 percent of total equity in Puerto Rican banks in 2004, compared with just 1 percent in the United States (see table 8-3). They also note that in the five more aggressive banks, disproportionately large securities holdings with ten-year maturities appear to have been mismatched with five-year maximum debt, leading to significant problems, which in 2005 resulted in declines in their stock prices. The need for a well-developed interest rate risk management strategy seems apparent.

Table 8-2. *Asset Composition of Commercial Banks as Share of Total Assets, Puerto Rico, Selected Years, 1995–2004*
Percent, except as indicated

Item	1995	2000	2004	CAGR[a]
Investments and securities	31.3	39.7	41.1	16.2
Loans secured by residential real estate	13.8	15.4	19.0	16.8
Loans secured by other real estate	9.2	10.0	11.6	15.7
Commercial and industrial loans	17.8	15.1	14.1	9.8
Other assets	5.6	3.9	3.7	7.8
Cash and interest-bearing placements	5.0	3.5	3.6	8.9
Other loans and leases, net	0.2	1.0	0.5	23.3
Loans to individuals	17.1	11.4	6.4	1.1
Total assets	100	100	100	12.8
Total assets (millions of dollars)	31,969	54,785	94,330	. . .

Source: Data from the Office of the Commissioner of Financial Institutions of Puerto Rico.
a. Cumulative annual growth rate, 1995–2004.

Table 8-3. *Liability and Equity Composition of Commercial Banks as Share of Total Assets, Puerto Rico, Selected Years, 1995–2004*
Percent, except as indicated

Item	1995	2000	2004	CAGR[a]
Liabilities	92.7	93.6	93.4	12.9
Brokered deposits	0.0	8.0	13.5	40.9
Advances from the Federal Home Loan Bank	0.0	8.5	7.4	57.0
Section 936 deposits	15.4	3.2	0.0	−100.0
Total deposits (excluding section 936 and brokered)	58.3	47.7	36.1	6.9
Long-term debt	4.4	3.9	12.0	26.0
Short-term debt	12.4	19.9	19.4	18.6
Other liabilities	2.3	2.6	4.9	22.9
Equity	7.3	6.4	6.6	11.5
Preferred stock	0.1	0.2	0.4	37.2
Other equity	7.2	6.2	6.2	10.8
Total liabilities and equity (percent)	100	100	100	12.8
Total liabilities and equity (millions of dollars)	31,969	54,785	94,330	. . .

Source: Data from the Office of the Commissioner of Financial Institutions of Puerto Rico.
a. Cumulative annual growth rate, 1995–2004, computed using first nonzero entry.

International Banking Entities (IBEs) in Puerto Rico

There were some thirty-five IBEs operating in Puerto Rico at the end of 2004. In their examination of these institutions' ownership assets, offshore operations, and regulation, the authors find that while IBE assets have doubled in the last decade, IBEs have not increased employment on the island to any measurable degree, and have not sufficiently attracted real investors to Puerto Rico. Moreover, the regulation of the law governing IBEs leaves much to be desired, most particularly with regard to transparency. An important, independent outside review of the IBE sector is detailed in the chapter. It includes several well-reasoned conclusions and recommendations to the government.

Insurance Companies

As in the mainland states, there is a local regulator of the insurance sector on the island, in this case the Office of the Commissioner of Insurance. Data on the extent of the role of the 312 insurance companies in Puerto Rico (some 50 domestic and 262 international) indicate that their current 6 percent share of total financial system assets is down from 9 percent in 1995. The authors indicate that this is a sector in transition because, since the passage of the 1999 U.S. Gramm-Leach-Bliley Act, insurance and banking are no longer completely separated under Puerto Rican law.

Other Financial Institutions

The much smaller, though relevant, financial system roles of the 41 investment companies (mutual funds), 50 mortgage companies, 140 credit unions, 46 finance companies, 9 broker-dealer and leasing companies and small loan companies, as well as the dozen venture capital firms, are presented in detail. Some $26.2 billion in equities and fixed-income investment made up the volume of local funds saved by individuals and companies in 2004, a rather sizable amount for an island with allegedly negative savings. The authors note the possibility that there is a substantial amount of underground economy investment and even some double-counting. In volume, however, the assets of these institutions together are much less than the total assets of commercial banks.

Government Banks

The Government Development Bank (GDB) plays a significant role in the Puerto Rican financial system. The authors detail the history of the GDB from its inception in 1942. The GDB was created to serve as a fiscal agent

for the government, as a depository and trustee of government funds, as a
lender to the government and the private sector (not in competition with
private sector institutions), and importantly, as a financial adviser to the
governor and public agencies, corporations, and instrumentalities, including
municipalities. The principal role of the GDB today is to operate in the
dynamic and competitive financial markets in the United States as bond
issuer/market creator, maintaining the flow of information about Puerto
Rico for the benefit of the United States and international investment communities. The GDB is not solely a fiscal agent, however. It is responsible for
serving as a watchdog with regard to the way public funds are spent. It also
advises the governor, the Puerto Rico Office of Management and Budget,
and Puerto Rico's Treasury Department, among others, in developing economic initiatives and assists in the formulation and implementation of
financial solutions that facilitate the development and execution of Puerto
Rico's fiscal policy.

The authors present a comprehensive analysis of the GDB's financial
statements, its bond flotations ($51.7 billion from April 1993 to June
2004), and its use of the funds raised. In summary, $34.4 billion of new
money was raised for investment in government projects and $17.2 billion
for refunding outstanding debt, producing net savings of $204.5 million
during this ten-year period.

The GDB has official subsidiaries such as the Housing Finance Authority
(PRHFA), which assists low- and moderate-income families with house
building and improvement, as well as "social interest" housing creation for
the neediest families; the Puerto Rico Tourism Development Fund, which
provides both investment and partial and total guarantees to privately
financed tourism related projects; the Puerto Rico Development Fund,
which was created to undertake capital investments via common or preferred stocks in enterprises that are judged to significantly contribute to economic growth but that are unable to obtain private funding; a capital fund
to facilitate the GDB's own investment activities; and the Puerto Rico
Finance Corporation, which provides alternative financing operations to
agencies and instrumentalities of the government.

The authors also review the GDB's affiliation with four other governmental organizations with regard to financing and administrative and technical assistance: the Puerto Rico Industrial, Tourist, Educational, Medical
and Environmental Control Financing Authority (AFICA); the Puerto Rico
Infrastructure Financing Authority (PRIFA); the Puerto Rico Municipal
Finance Agency (PRMFA), and the Caribbean Projects Financing Authority
(CARIFA). Finally, there are thirteen other Commonwealth of Puerto Rico

corporations that the GDB assists with bond issues, interim financing, and other services, including the Puerto Rico Aqueduct and Sewer Authority, the sole provider of water and sewer services on the island.

This broad array of relationships with internal and external affiliated institutions illustrates the ubiquitous presence of the GDB and its crucial role in the long-term financing and direct lending to the government sector in Puerto Rico. The GDB plays a key role in obtaining access to the U.S. municipal bond markets. The GDB's activities are also intertwined with those of other government agencies to which it provides administrative and technical assistance in many areas.

The authors conclude that, on balance, the GDB has been an effective financial presence in the island. However, the GDB and Puerto Rico presently face quite sizable problems. The public debt is listed as $33.9 billion. However, this figure does not include the current shortfall in Puerto Rico's five government retirement systems. That underfunded amount is estimated at an additional $3.8 to $11.8 billion. Despite the plethora of data in the chapter, complete data in some areas of financial operations are still quite difficult to obtain. What is clear, however, is that the central government has been borrowing against future tax revenues. An important example is the amount borrowed directly from the GDB itself in order to satisfy the legal requirement that the budget be balanced: some $233 million on a ten-year term for FY 2003; $370 million for FY 2004; $550 million for FY 2005—all debt to be repaid by tax receivables. In addition, a $500 million line of credit from the GDB's equity will finance the recently established Special Communities Perpetual Trust.

Therefore, willingly or not, the GDB has some—even if tangential—responsibility for the increase in the public debt and the related problems of vast increases in government bureaucracy. In this context, it is important to note that on May 19, 2005, Moody's ratings service downgraded Commonwealth of Puerto Rico general obligation bonds to Baa2 from Baa1 and kept the rating outlook negative.[1] On May 24, 2005, Standard and Poor's cut the bond rating to BBB from A–. Both moves were due to concerns about public expenditures growing faster than the economy, government spending in excess of revenues covered by borrowing, and government assignment of nonrecurrent funds to key investment projects.[2]

The GDB's capacity to be an effective and efficient government policy planner and adviser is severely hampered by its political dependence on the

1. Moody's Investors Service, Global Credit Research (2005).
2. Standard and Poor's (2005).

governor's power of appointment and discharge. During the first twenty-eight years of the GDB's existence (1942–69) there were only four presidents, who served an average of seven years per term. However over the next thirty-five, despite one eight-year presidential term (1978–85), the average term of the fifteen presidents was less than 2.5 years. Of those, the five most recent presidents have a modern tenure of less than 1.5 years. This is hardly time enough to develop any muscle, much less flex it. The authors also discuss the role of the other government bank: the Economic Development Bank (EDB). While not unimportant, it is both secondary to the GDB and subject to the same political power weaknesses.

Benchmarking

In the penultimate section of the chapter, the authors benchmark Puerto Rico's financial system against that of the United States They compare Puerto Rico's banking sector with that on the mainland and in two states (Florida and Hawaii).

The authors conclude that the contribution of the financial, insurance, and real estate sectors (FIRE) to economic activity in Puerto Rico can be favorably compared with that in the mainland United States during the period 1947 to 2004. The U.S. mainland maintains data for the FIRE sector in the national income accounts, while for Puerto Rico these data are available in the commonwealth GDP accounts. The data series, national income (NI) and gross domestic product (GDP), are not strictly comparable, although they are useful in evaluating the contribution of the FIRE sector to overall economic activity. The FIRE contribution to NI in the United States increased from 9 percent to 19 percent, while in Puerto Rico it increased from 9 percent to 17 percent during the period. The overall activity of Puerto Rico's financial sector has roughly kept pace with that of the United States. Throughout the period, the differential between the two data series was between 1 and 4 percentage points.

In their comparisons, the authors highlight three points. First, investments in securities among banks in Puerto Rico are much higher (37 percent) than in the United States (18 percent), Florida (18 percent), and Hawaii (21 percent) and increased by 10 percentage points over the period compared with 0.2 percentage points in the United States as a whole and 2 percentage points in both Florida and Hawaii. Second, total deposits as a percentage of assets were lower in Puerto Rico than in the benchmark regions: 61 percent versus 67 percent in the United States as a whole, 80 percent in Florida, and 71 percent in Hawaii. Assets funded by deposits declined by 19 percentage points in Puerto Rico over the period, as against declines of 4 percentage points in the United States and 2 percentage points in Florida and an increase of 9 percentage points in Hawaii. Third, there was a significant increase in Puerto Rican banks' debt relative to that of the benchmarks: debt in Puerto Rico was 32 percent of total assets, 24 percent in the United States, 11 percent in Florida, and 19 percent in Hawaii. Debt finance increased by 19 percentage points in Puerto Rico over the nine-year period as against 3 percentage points in the United States as a whole and 1 percentage point in Florida, whereas Hawaii actually experienced a decline of 13 percentage points in bank assets financed by debt. Finally, banks in Puerto Rico have a lower proportion of equity to total assets (7 percent versus 9 percent in both the United States as a whole and in Florida, and 10 percent in Hawaii). The ratio of equity to total assets has declined in Puerto Rico but increased in all of the benchmark regions.

Summary of Principal Recommendations

The Puerto Rican financial system has achieved much, but is in need of improvement if the island is to realize its economic potential. Drawing from their work, the authors advance an extensive list of recommendations, grouped into six distinct areas. Their key points are summarized below.

Commercial Banks

Maldonado-Bear and Walter conclude that Puerto Rico needs to increase funds allocated to economic development via commercial and industrial loans. This could be achieved through reallocation as well as expansion, in their view preferably through enhancing growth in household deposits. They argue that all banks must do a better job of balancing the trade-off between dedicating funds for development and for more liquid investment such as securities, particularly from governments and instrumentalities. However, they note that problems related to fragile financial structure, such as debt equity composition, appear to be concentrated in five specific banks.

They advocate amending Puerto Rico's Internal Revenue Code as it applies to financial institutions, in order to eliminate the multiple income tax exemptions on investment of several types (local government issues or the U.S. government and its agencies' issues). Such exemptions tend to make it more profitable for banks to allocate funds to these investments than to lend for industrial and commercial development. Several types of income from local real estate loans are exempt as well, further inducing banks to allocate funds to real estate as their second major asset group and hence less to commercial and industrial loans and loans to individuals.

International Banking Entities

They advocate implementing several of the key recommendations in the tax policy area suggested by outside evaluation and analysis groups to the Commissioner of Financial Institutions. These include exempting the taxation of income from offshore operations within Puerto Rico, together with overall tax law improvements aimed at achieving uniformity and consistency. In their view, the current approach allows the commissioner overly broad discretion in setting the tax rates applicable to IBEs, and results in tax rulings that are often opaque.

Other Financial Institutions

Investment companies, broker-dealers, and the few venture capital funds operating have generally laudable financial intermediation records. However, the authors believe that more could be done to promote cooperation and interaction with authorities and to educate the public in order to channel more savings to those institutions.

Government Development Bank

The authors propose that presidential terms be lengthened to seven years in both the GDB and the Economic Development Bank, and that both banks include board representation from each group represented in the Puerto Rican financial sector. They also support empowering the GDB to issue stock and sell it to commercial banks and other financial institutions. They stress that these and other proposals do not aim to divert power from the executive or the legislature to the GDB, which could become a constitutional issue. Rather, they are meant to encourage the GDB president to be a positive, expert source of policy guidance.

Retirement Systems

The various government pension plans should be brought to financial health by legislative revenue allocations, with assets to be invested in securities of diverse industries and geographic locations. Puerto Rico might then consider the positive experience of several developing countries in using healthy retirement systems as guarantors of private industrial development loans.

Financial Statistics

Proposals here focus on measures to improve the quality of Puerto Rican statistics and strengthen the technology for gathering, storing, and disseminating information. The authors stress that accurate and accessible data are of critical importance, not only to the government, but to researchers and the general public as well.

In his commentary, Arturo Estrella stressed that the relatively short annual series preclude an analytic assessment of many questions of interest. For instance, financial developments on the mainland may be more important than those locally for explaining Puerto Rico's economic growth. And in developing their policy recommendations, the authors do not attempt to assess how special features of Puerto Rico's financial system influence the choice of policy tools.

James Hanson argued that Puerto Rico's special attachments to the United States have broader and deeper implications for its financial system than those addressed by the authors. In his view these links may help to explain special features of the island's banking system, such as the relatively low local deposits. They also suggest that Puerto Rico can do little to further increase the size of its banking system. Hanson cautioned that GDB loans to the private sector need not imply that the receiving firms were unable to borrow privately, as the chapter authors conclude, but may instead reflect subsidies. More broadly, he noted that empirical evidence suggests that large state banks have tended to depress growth rates, and that an independent assessment of the efficiency and transparency of GDB activities would be desirable.

9

Trade Performance and Industrial Policy

ROBERT Z. LAWRENCE AND JUAN LARA

Puerto Rico has a small but extremely open economy. Thus its trade—both with the mainland and with the rest of the world—is a central determinant of its economic performance. In this chapter, Robert Lawrence and Juan Lara consider some of the issues related to Puerto Rican trade performance, focusing on implications for external adjustment and domestic employment and growth. In addition, they analyze the strengths and weaknesses of Puerto Rican industrial policy and present policy recommendations to improve Puerto Rico's trade performance.

The Relevance of Trade Performance

Trade performance is of interest for at least two distinct reasons. The first relates to the external constraint. For most economies, there are both monetary and real dimensions to external adjustment. Countries need imported components and capital to grow. While these purchases can be financed temporarily through borrowing, in the long run they have to be paid for by exports or capital inflows such as foreign direct investment. If exports fail to grow fast enough to meet import needs, relative price adjustments brought about through changes in the real exchange rate may be required.

But Puerto Rico has a fixed exchange rate and is part of the U.S. monetary system. The dollar is both its domestic and its foreign currency. This means that exchange rate adjustment plays a relatively minor role in external adjustment. If Puerto Ricans have unsustainable spending patterns, they will eventually be forced to adjust. Such adjustments might, to be sure, involve not only changes in income and spending by private citizens and the commonwealth government, but also require shifts in relative prices. But these will occur directly through product and factor price adjustments rather than changes in the exchange rate.

The second reason trade performance is of interest is its relationship to domestic performance, in particular employment and growth. Puerto Rico has had a high and persistent unemployment rate—12.5 percent in October 2005—and very low labor force participation rates. In particular, employment growth in Puerto Rican manufacturing, which is closely linked to trade performance, has been weak. Between 2000 and December 2004, for example, Puerto Rican manufacturing employment declined by almost 20 percent. The labor market appears to be in long-run disequilibrium, and it is difficult to reduce real wages to clear the market because of U.S. social transfers and minimum wage and immigration policies. Given these constraints, it is natural to think of measures that could shift the demand curve for labor outward, which better trade performance might do.

The other dimension of domestic performance relates to growth. There is a strong correlation between trade and economic growth with causal linkages running both ways, and thus trade performance may be particularly important not only in shifting the composition of output toward sectors with strong growth potential but also in stimulating investment and productivity growth.

Using official data, figure 9-1 highlights some striking trends in Puerto Rico's trade balances. The merchandise trade surplus is large and growing. Indeed, exports of goods (not shown) were over 75 percent of GDP in 2003. This surplus is more than offset by the deficit in services trade, reflecting payments of profits earned by foreign corporations (39 percent of GDP in 2003). However, measurement issues and data limitations make it difficult to construct a complete picture of Puerto Rico's balance of payments.

Puerto Rico's External Constraint

As part of their analysis, the authors estimated a pair of trade equations using annual data from 1975 to 2003 to explain Puerto Rican exports and

Figure 9-1. *Balance of Payments, Puerto Rico, 1989–2003*
Percent

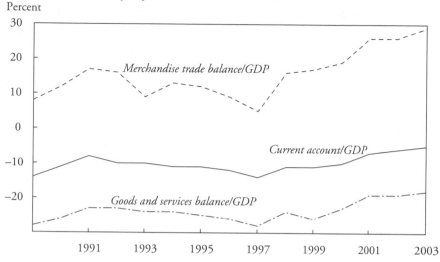

Source: Data from U.S. Department of Commerce; Puerto Rican Planning Board.

imports of goods during that period. They use U.S. GDP to capture the export market, since more than 80 percent of Puerto Rico's exports go to the United States; and for the relative price of exports they used a ratio of the implicit Puerto Rican export price deflator and the U.S. import price index. For imports they use Puerto Rican GDP as the income variable and the ratio of the Puerto Rican implicit import price deflator to the personal consumption expenditure deflator.

Lawrence and Lara find that each 1 percent growth in real U.S. GDP results in a 2 percent rise in Puerto Rican export volumes. In contrast, they find that each 1 percent increase in Puerto Rican GDP results in a 1.26 percent rise in the volume of Puerto Rican imports. Interpreted structurally, therefore, this pair of equations suggest that if these historic relationships held and if Puerto Rican GDP growth were 58 percent faster (that is, 2/1.26 = 1.58) than GDP growth in the United States, imports would rise as rapidly as exports. In fact between 1993 and 2002, Puerto Rican and U.S. GDP grew at 4.1 and 3.2 percent respectively, a ratio of 1.28. With constant relative prices, therefore, these coefficients imply that with these growth rates there would be a strong trend toward a trade surplus, since Puerto Rican exports and imports would grow at 8.2 and 4.0 percent per year respectively.

In recent years, Puerto Rican exports have grown very rapidly. Between 1999 and 2003, Puerto Rican exports to countries outside the United States grew by 44 percent when total U.S. exports increased by just 4 percent. Only three states or regions recorded faster export growth (Washington, D.C. (96 percent), Nevada (90 percent), and South Carolina (65 percent). Similarly the $3.6 billion increase in the dollar value of Puerto Rican exports was exceeded only by Texas ($15.6 billion), Ohio ($4.9 billion), and South Carolina ($4.6 billion). In a period in which most U.S. exporters were hurt by the strong dollar and slow global economic growth, this was a particularly impressive performance.

In general terms, therefore, the analysis of Puerto Rican trade performance suggests that it is not a constraint on the island's growth. Relative price adjustments are not therefore required to maintain external balance. Indeed, using the official export and import data, the analysis suggests that Puerto Rican GDP growth could exceed that of the mainland before import growth would equal export growth. With the relatively slower growth differential Puerto Rico has actually recorded, the trade surplus has increased.

However, the authors point out that there are concerns about the data on which this analysis rests. Tax considerations provide international firms with incentives to overstate their Puerto Rican activities. This means that the export data may not give an accurate picture of the value that is actually added in the Commonwealth, and in particular the data could distort the employment implications of trade flows. The authors explore this issue by adjusting exports for foreign profits and directly examining employment growth. They find that the positive impressions of trade performance survive these adjustments.

The authors also empirically explore the extent to which Puerto Rico's exports are vulnerable to U.S. trade liberalization. This is a potential concern because the United States is by far its largest trading partner. Reductions in tariff barriers, for example to countries that sign free trade agreements, erode Puerto Rico's unique access to the U.S. market. However, they conclude that the Commonwealth's exports to the mainland are not dependent on tariff preferences and are thus unlikely to be affected by further liberalization.

Puerto Rico's Comparative Advantage

The authors then proceed to explore the microeconomic dimensions of export performance. Their analysis points to the overwhelming role U.S. tax policy has played in determining Puerto Rico's comparative advantage. As shown in table 9-1, the Commonwealth has become increasingly specialized in high-tech products such as pharmaceuticals, which when produced in the

Table 9-1. *Main Puerto Rican Exports, 2003*
Units as indicated

Description	HTS code	Percent of exports to the United States	Percent of exports to the rest of the world
Pharmaceutical products	30	56.9	40.2
Nuclear reactors, boilers, machinery, and mechanical appliances	84	7.8	21.5
Organic chemicals	29	8.2	13.1
Optical, photographic, cinematographic, measuring, checking, precision, medical, and surgical instruments	90	9.3	4.2
Total		85.7	79.0

Source: Data from Puerto Rico Planning Board.

mainland United States require intensive skilled labor, capital, and research and development. Puerto Rico sells these products in astounding volumes both to the United States and to other developed economies.

Whatever may have been the original reasons for locating in Puerto Rico, the high-tech sectors in Puerto Rico have now established a firm footing in the Commonwealth. Despite the repeal of section 936 of the 1976 Tax Reform Act, growth in these sectors has been sustained; indeed it has accelerated. The process appears to have become self-reinforcing, even if the connections with the rest of the economy are not deep. In particular there has been robust employment growth in the pharmaceuticals sector since the section 936 tax provisions were repealed. In addition, there is evidence of smaller but rapidly growing services exports that are more closely linked to Puerto Rican factor endowments.

In order to understand this dynamic, Lawrence and Lara analyze the unit values of products that Puerto Rico sells to the United States and to the rest of the world, as well as the characteristics of Puerto Rican exports in terms of production inputs. To undertake this exercise they collected data for the year 2000 for U.S. manufacturing on average compensation, which would produce a measure of labor skills; profits as a share of value added, which indicates (tangible and intangible) capital intensity; and the share of scientists and engineers per 1,000 employees, which indicates R&D intensity.

In the United States in 2000, average annual compensation in manufacturing was $53,807. However, weighting each three-digit NAICS manufacturing sector compensation by the value of its exports gives an average

Table 9-2. *Measures of Input Intensity of Puerto Rican Exports, 2000*[a]

Units as indicated

Sector	Skill[b]	Capital[c]	R&D[d]
(1) U.S. manufacturing	53,807	0.37	45
(2) Puerto Rican exports	66,427	0.47	83
(3) U.S. exports	64,539	0.31	87
Ratios			
(2)/(3) Puerto Rican exports / U.S. exports	1.03	1.52	0.96
(2)/(1) Puerto Rican exports / U.S. manufacturing	1.23	1.27	1.83
(3)/(1) U.S exports / U.S. manufacturing	1.20	0.83	1.92

Source: National Science Foundation, *Annual Survey of Manufactures,* IO tables.

a. In each sector, 2000 U.S. input measures are weighted by industry output.

b. Skill refers to average compensation per worker in U.S. dollars.

c. Capital refers to the share of profits in value added.

d. R&D refers to the number of scientists and engineers per 1,000 employees.

compensation of $64,539, suggesting that workers in U.S. manufactured exports are 20 percent more skilled than in manufacturing as a whole. As shown in table 9-2, aggregating the U.S. compensation measures using Puerto Rican manufactured goods exports for 2000 as weights leads to an estimate of $66,427, suggesting, *on the basis of U.S. input coefficients,* that Puerto Rican manufactured goods exports are actually more skill intensive than U.S. manufactured goods exports. Remarkably, however, if they were produced using U.S. input ratios, Puerto Rican exports would be only slightly less concentrated in R&D-intensive sectors than U.S. exports. This is particularly noteworthy since the authors also find that U.S. exports are much more highly concentrated in R&D-intensive sectors (1.92) than U.S. manufacturing output. They also find that Puerto Rican exports have much higher capital-intensity measures. *In sum, compared with U.S. exports, Puerto Rican exports are slightly more skill intensive, slightly less R&D intensive, and far more capital intensive.*

According to the authors' analysis, the reason for this is that foreign firms have been attracted to Puerto Rico not by the traditional advantages that it might have been expected to provide (or might once have provided), such as a relatively abundant labor endowment or duty-free access to the U.S. market. Instead, the real benefits stem from being able to enjoy the advantages that the U.S. tax code provides to U.S. corporations that operate in the commonwealth and the agglomeration economies that these activities appear to have created.

These advantages are greatest where firms can take advantage of transfer pricing opportunities to undervalue the transfer of intellectual property obtained in the United States. They also confer an advantage on capital-intensive operations. *The result is that Puerto Rico is competitive in products that paradoxically reflect mainland comparative advantages in high-technology activities.* Another result is an export sector that is made up of large foreign-owned firms and is not deeply integrated into the local economy. At the same time, however, this is clearly a dynamic activity that has continued to flourish in recent years despite the elimination of the even more favorable treatment that was provided under the section 936 tax provisions.

Services

In contrast to Puerto Rican exports of goods, Puerto Rican services exports, which have recently been growing rapidly, appear more grounded in the island's factor endowments. To be sure, the Commonwealth has provided some modest tax incentives to stimulate this activity, but it appears to have arisen more organically from developments in the domestic economy. There are a large number of well-educated Puerto Ricans who earn substantially less than their U.S. counterparts. In addition, Puerto Rico has a dynamic domestic financial sector that enjoys participation in an economy based on the U.S. dollar and is subject to U.S. regulatory oversight. The Spanish language also gives Puerto Rican service providers a natural advantage in Central and Latin America.

Puerto Rican Imports

The authors also examine Puerto Rican imports. A significant share of these imports consists of capital goods and inputs into imports. In general, the goods imported from the mainland United States are very different from those imported from the rest of the world, and for the most part have quite different characteristics from goods produced in and exported from the commonwealth.

The authors compute the factor content of imports, again using U.S. input coefficients for both Puerto Rico and the United States. As shown in table 9-3, they find that weighting each industry's input coefficients by Puerto Rican import weights suggests that the goods Puerto Rico imports are relatively more skill intensive (13 percent), capital intensive (19 percent), and especially R&D intensive (38 percent) than U.S. manufacturing as a whole. Imports to both Puerto Rico and the United States are produced with quite similar compensation levels, but Puerto Rican imports tend to be substantially more capital intensive (ratio 1.45) and less R&D intensive than

Table 9-3. *Measures of Input Intensity of Puerto Rican Imports, 2000*[a]
Units as indicated

Sector	Skill[b]	Capital[c]	R&D[d]
(1) U.S. manufacturing	53,807	0.37	45
(2) Puerto Rican imports	60,865	0.44	63
(3) U.S. imports	61,317	0.31	77
Ratios			
(2)/(3) Puerto Rican imports / U.S. imports	0.99	1.45	0.82
(2)/(1) Puerto Rican imports / U.S. manufacturing	1.13	1.19	1.38
(3)/(1) U.S. imports / U.S. manufacturing	1.14	0.82	1.69

Source: National Science Foundation, *Annual Survey of Manufactures*, IO tables.
a. In each case, 2000 U.S. inputs are weighted by the indicated sectoral output.
b. Skill refers to average compensation per worker in U.S. dollars.
c. Capital refers to the share of profits in value added.
d. R&D refers to the number of scientists and engineers per 1,000 employees.

U.S. imports. This profile might suggest Puerto Rico is about as skill intensive as the United States, less capital intensive, and more R&D intensive.

However, the authors point out that, owing to the high level of aggregation at which this exercise is carried out, these results should be taken with a large grain of salt. It also suggests that Puerto Rico might need considerable investment in skills, capital, and R&D to accomplish a significant amount of import substitution because Puerto Rico imports a relatively small share of more basic commodities.

Policy Recommendations

The authors note that as an economy that is part of the U.S. monetary system and subject to the U.S. customs regime, Puerto Rico can have neither an independent exchange rate policy nor an independent trade policy. Industrial policy is therefore one of the few policy instruments the commonwealth has at its disposal. The empirical part of the paper suggests that Puerto Rican growth is not constrained by its external performance and that therefore the focus of Puerto Rican industrial policies should be on stimulating growth.

The authors, however, emphasize the need for caution in the use of industrial policies. Policymakers should intervene only in those situations where they can demonstrate that the overall gains to Puerto Rico would exceed those obtained by private decisionmakers. Efforts to provide broad incentives are likely to be costly and wasteful in that they will encourage activities that would have been undertaken in the absence of the policy. It is important to be clear that the mere fact that a product is being purchased from a domestic source rather than imported does not make the purchase preferable. Likewise, the fact that money is being given to small rather than large firms or that money goes to one sector rather than another does not make it preferable. *The crucial issue is whether an activity that is being promoted is likely to have social benefits beyond those that the individual entrepreneur can capture.*

Some analysts have expressed deep dissatisfaction with the Puerto Rican model of growth and trade because it has emphasized foreign investment and exports and failed to involve large parts of the population. They advocate a more active policy of import substitution.[1] Lawrence and Lara argue that it is not obvious that such a policy focus can succeed in today's world economy. Instead, the authors believe that it is more reasonable to think about policies that promote innovation, learning, and coordination throughout the economy.[2] Some of these would entail assisting activities that predominate in tradable goods and could build on two distinct opportunities: the dynamic high-tech sector clusters in Puerto Rico and services exports both to the United States and to the Western Hemisphere. At the same time, opportunities in sectors that are not involved in trade should not be neglected.

In principle, the government could have a role to play in three crucial areas—stimulating innovation and social learning; aiding in the collective coordination of investments; and providing public goods and infrastructure—because these activities are unlikely to be provided in optimal quantities by private individuals acting alone. Industrial policy would thus be best implemented by promoting these activities throughout the economy. But it is also important that the government be able to apply such policies effectively. Government failure could be worse than market failure.[3]

Recent Puerto Rican industrial policies have emphasized the promotion of clusters particularly in the high-tech sector and exports more generally. There are some examples in which policy does seem to be aimed at dealing with market failures and improving public infrastructure, but other areas in which the approach remains undeveloped or lacks focus and is therefore likely to be wasteful. An approach that narrows the scope to dealing only with clear cases of market failure is likely to give better results.

The authors believe that there is room for improvement in the provision of adequate infrastructure and public goods by the government in Puerto

1. See Dietz (2003).
2. See Hausmann and Rodrik (2003).
3. See Rodrik (2004).

Rico, a fact most government officials readily accept. The island is better
stocked with transportation, communications, power, and water infrastructure than most developing countries, but it still does not measure up to
developed-country standards in many respects. The water and sewage system in particular is severely hampered by underinvestment and poor labor-
management relations. The supply of electric power is adequate, but costs
much more than on the mainland and in many other countries. The network of roads and highways crisscrosses the whole island, but it has deteriorated and is severely congested in many areas. These problems impose costs
on productive activities and restrictions on future development, which
means that every dollar invested in their solution is likely to generate substantial private and social returns.

As for the provision of public goods, a top concern of Puerto Rican
authorities should be to improve public safety. This is not only a primary
social objective, but also a necessary condition for the maintenance of
an attractive business environment. Like most countries, Puerto Rico is
afflicted with a rising crime rate, largely related to drug trafficking and drug
addiction. Reversing that trend is a major challenge for the authorities and
Puerto Rican society in general. It is also necessary to strengthen the educational system, especially at the basic and middle levels and particularly in the
areas serving lower-income groups.

In the specific area of export promotion, government policy has also
been trying to play the role of facilitator rather than picking winners. The
export promotion agency has emphasized the provision of market intelli-
gence to actual and potential exporters, which may be seen as a "public
good." The agency also devotes a good deal of its resources to helping local
firms participate in trade fairs and trade missions, thus performing a necessary coordination function.

A more controversial practice—with more uncertain potential outcomes—
is the targeting and nurturing of local firms to help them become exporters,
which has been frequently advocated by both business and government lead-
ers. This has not been the main thrust of the export promotion agency, but
more because of budget constraints than choice of strategy. It can be argued
that Puerto Rico's industrial and export promotion policies are increasingly
moving in the right direction, but elements of older policies still play an
important role. For example, in recent years local authorities have been
stressing preferential government procurement practices to stimulate local
businesses. Legislation was enacted in 2002 to set aside a portion of public
sector purchases exclusively for local suppliers, and more recently the administration of Governor Anibal Acevedo Vilá has expressed its support for the

law and its intention to ensure that it is faithfully enforced. This is a form of import substitution that could run afoul of regional trade agreements between the United States and several Caribbean and Latin American countries. But even if such legal problems could be avoided, there is still a danger that automatic preferences for local suppliers may lead to rent seeking instead of promoting new investment and to expenditures that are wasteful.

In his comments, James Dietz had a more negative perspective on the recent performance of the Puerto Rican economy, viewing the low employment rate as reflective of a large waste of human resources. He suggested additional research to explore the link between export growth and local employment. He pointed to the strong performance of exports since elimination of the section 936 tax incentives, and asked whether greater emphasis should have been given to the strong growth of the pharmaceutical industry on both the mainland and Puerto Rico. For the future, he argued that attention should be given to expanding the links between mainland and local firms. Daniel Lederman argued that all of the contributors to the volume should have viewed Puerto Rico more from the perspective of economic development, particularly its deep economic integration with the United States, and placed emphasis on the tax incentive issues. While he was generally sympathetic to some of the proposals of Lawrence and Lara for industrial policy, he suggested the need for a means of monitoring and evaluating such policies.

10

Restoring Growth: The Policy Options

BARRY P. BOSWORTH AND SUSAN M. COLLINS

In the middle of the twentieth century, Puerto Rico emerged as one of the world's fastest-growing economies, drawing comparisons with the rapidly industrializing countries of East Asia. Over the past several decades, however, while the economy has continued to grow, it has done so at a greatly reduced rate. Since 1980, there has been no further convergence of living standards with those of the U.S. mainland. Income per capita is currently only 30 percent of the U.S. average, and 58 percent of all children live below the U.S. poverty level.

Identifying the causes of Puerto Rico's deteriorating economic performance has been a primary objective of this project, and it is an important backdrop for designing a turnaround strategy. Drawing on the prior chapters, we argue in the following section that in terms of providing an environment conducive to growth, Puerto Rico can be characterized as a glass that is only half full. Furthermore, while its unique position vis-à-vis the United States provides it with valuable opportunities and advantages, this position also creates constraints and disincentives that are particularly intransigent. From this perspective, we summarize our assessment of the main factors behind the island's growth slowdown. These factors are clearly

interrelated and interact in complex ways. Thus it would be extremely difficult to pin down the relative importance of each, and it is not our objective
to do so.

Similarly, in developing a growth strategy we argue against seeking a single answer, proposing instead a program that addresses each of the major
problem areas. That strategy is outlined in some detail in the second section.
Its primary focus is a set of measures aimed at addressing Puerto Rico's most
evident problem, a low employment rate for its adult population. The proposals include greater incentives to seek employment and actions to expand
the range of private sector job opportunities. Puerto Rico must also act
quickly to shore up its education system—an area of previously strong performance that has begun to experience greater problems. If it is to succeed in
the future, prosperity will be built on the structure of a well-educated and
productive workforce. Finally, there is an important need to improve governance by increasing the transparency of government decisions and reducing
the tendency to use government powers to restrict competition and promote
rent-seeking behavior.

Puerto Rico has few if any natural resources, and any advantages it has
realized from a special relationship with the United States are quickly being
eroded. It is also important to recognize that neither traditional tourism nor
low-wage manufacturing offer viable ways forward. Puerto Rico requires a
dynamic, modern, outward-oriented economy that attracts international
businesses and the job opportunities that they offer.

Diagnosing the Growth Slowdown

This section provides the context for the policy prescriptions that follow.
We begin by summarizing what we believe to be the main lessons about economic growth that can be distilled from the economics literature. We then
assess how Puerto Rico's economy measures up from this vantage point.
Given the prior decades of successful performance, understanding what
went wrong in the past quarter century is critical. Thus the final part of the
section takes a somewhat broader historical perspective so as to outline why
growth slowed.

Basic Growth Determinants

The effort to understand the determinants of economic growth has generated an enormous volume of economic research. Even a casual perusal of
this work makes clear that views about the economic (and other) characteris-

tics that are most critical for growth have evolved over time. Furthermore, neither the theoretical nor the empirical studies point to a simple, cookie-cutter listing of necessary or sufficient conditions. Nonetheless, emerging from this work is an underlying core set of policy objectives that most analysts believe can create an environment conducive to both accelerating and sustaining economic growth. That core set can be divided into four broad policy groupings of: macroeconomic stability, openness, institutions and the business climate, and physical and human capital.

Macroeconomic stability refers to an integrated mix of a sustainable fiscal program and sound monetary policies. On the fiscal side, budget deficits should be small enough to ensure manageable levels of debt and required debt service; tax revenues should be adequate to provide the government with the resources to achieve its expenditure goals; and spending allocations should be consistent with those goals. With an increased awareness of the distorting effects of high tax rates on economic decisions, emphasis is placed on the combination of a broad tax base and low rates. Monetary policy should focus on maintaining low inflation and a competitive exchange rate.

Openness involves the interaction with the external global economy, with a particular emphasis on openness of the trade regime. Openness is particularly important to small economies, such as Puerto Rico, because of the opportunities that it offers to specialize in particular economic activities and to avoid the diseconomies of small-scale production. Competition in a larger economic arena also promotes efficiency and exposure to a wider range of innovations and other ideas. Openness includes financial interactions, such as inflows of foreign direct investment, that reduce the cost of capital for new investment and provide a channel for the spread of technology.

The importance of institutions for economic development has long been recognized. Their role was emphasized in the eighteenth-century writings of Adam Smith and more recently in the awarding of a Nobel Prize to the economist Douglass North. They have been a particular focus of research over the past decade aimed at determining which types of institutions are most important and the process through which they affect economic growth. In this literature, institutions are defined as the "rules of the game" that govern political, social, and economic interactions. Good institutions are those that create an incentive structure that reduces uncertainty and promotes economic efficiency. They protect individual initiative, promote trust by ensuring that promises will be kept, and constrain self-seeking political groups with rules that are enforced equally on everyone. Extensive efforts have been made to develop indicators of the quality of institutions of governance that focus on measures of corruption, political rights, regulatory burdens, and public sector efficiency.[1]

Finally, increases in physical capital per worker have long been seen as a major means of raising workers' productivity and incomes. The importance of capital has been further increased by a growing awareness of the need to define it broadly to include gains in educational attainment of the workforce and the development of new ideas that take the form of intangible capital. In the early stages of development, countries can make progress by simply using the technology of others: but as growth continues, reliance on external sources of capital and technology will yield diminishing returns in a world oversupplied with unskilled labor.

While these four factors can go a long way toward explaining the extraordinarily wide divergence of growth experiences over the past half century, the timing of the growth is more difficult to explain: What initiates a period of sustained growth? Why did countries like Ireland and the countries of East Asia, long mired in economic stagnation, achieve a transition to buoyant growth? Why did growth in Puerto Rico suddenly surge in the 1950s after many decades of abysmal poverty? Questions such as these are notoriously difficult to answer. However, the good news is that sustained increases in growth do not appear to be rare events. That growth accelerations appear to be much more common than typically recognized implies that they are achievable.[2]

Strengths and Concerns for Puerto Rico

At first blush, Puerto Rico looks extremely strong in terms of the four criteria discussed above, and its disappointing recent performance appears quite puzzling. The economy possesses many of the attributes that have emerged as key to fostering growth. The left side of table 10-1 lists a variety of ways in which the economy measures up favorably. In the macroeconomic arena, Puerto Rico operates completely within the U.S. monetary and financial system. In dealings with the mainland economy there are no risks of currency revaluations.

Furthermore, Puerto Rico is among the most open economies in the world. Located next to the world's largest market, it enjoys the unconstrained bilateral movement of goods, capital, and people. Trade in

1. Kaufmann, Kraay, and Zoido-Lobatón (2002).
2. Hausmann, Pritchett, and Rodrik (2004).

Table 10-1. *Strengths and Concerns for Puerto Rican Growth*

Factor	Strength	Concern or constraint
Macroeconomic	Stable currency Low inflation	Fiscal difficulties High and rising debt Lack of transparency No monetary independence
Openness	Access to U.S. markets, including financial markets Free flow of labor and capital Participant in U.S. open trade regime with rest of world Potential gateway to Latin American countries	U.S. law and treaties not designed for or by Puerto Rico Jones Act restrictions on trade with United States Exports poorly diversified
Institutions and business climate	Financial system access to mainland FDIC regulation of banks Legal system (including U.S. protection of intellectual property rights) U.S. social safety net	Complex and inconsistent tax policies Difficult regulatory procedures Political seesaw and policy uncertainty Poor incentive structure of transfer programs U.S. minimum wage U.S. dependency issues
Physical and human capital	High educational attainment English-speaking workforce Strong infrastructure for the region	Low investment, especially in the 1980s Concerns about school quality Weaknesses of the infrastructure compared with United States and Ireland Environmental degradation

goods and services operates within the U.S. customs union. Puerto Ricans are U.S. citizens and can travel and work freely on the mainland and change residence without restriction. Puerto Rico is also well situated to be a center for economic transactions within the Western Hemisphere and with Europe.

Third, the economic institutions of Puerto Rico are largely those of the United States. Economic activities in Puerto Rico are heavily guided by the U.S. legal and regulatory system. The commonwealth controls its own internal affairs, except where its authority is superseded by federal law.[3] As Rita Maldonado-Bear and Ingo Walter note, in chapter 8 of this volume, Puerto Rican enterprises and individuals have full access to U.S. financial markets, and its financial institutions are subject to the same supervisory oversight as mainland institutions. Thus in its economic affairs Puerto Rico is similar to a U.S. state, except for its exemption from the Internal Revenue Code. This provides a high degree of institutional certainty for doing business in Puerto Rico. In fact, Puerto Rico scores well on various international competitive indexes that aim to measure the quality of institutions.

Finally, as discussed in several of the prior chapters, Puerto Rico has achieved remarkable gains in the educational attainment of its population. The education level of the workforce today is comparable to that of the industrialized countries of the Organization for Economic Cooperation and Development. In the 2000 census, average years of schooling for the Puerto Rican population aged sixteen to sixty-four was 12.2 years compared with 13.8 years for the United States. Puerto Rico has a bilingual workforce, and the quality of its physical infrastructure is high compared with other countries in the region and relative to those with similar levels of income per capita.

However, as shown on the right side of table 10-1, an equal number of concerns may be constraining growth. In recent years, the government has had frequent fiscal problems. The public debt has been a rising percentage of revenues, and its bond ratings have been sharply lowered. Unlike many countries, Puerto Rico cannot use a currency devaluation to strengthen its competitive position. In addition, U.S. trade policies are not designed from the perspective of Puerto Rico's needs, and the island finds itself disadvantaged by laws that force it to use high-cost American shipping. Puerto Rico's trade is distorted and overly concentrated in a few areas in which American manufacturing was drawn to the island in pursuit of tax advantages that have now been eliminated. Furthermore, concerns have been raised that the

---

3. Puerto Rico is treated as a state for purposes of all federal legislation, with three important exceptions: income taxes, income support and welfare programs, and federal health care programs. In terms of economic affairs, federal legislation applies in all the important areas: agricultural standards, antitrust, aviation, banking, bankruptcy proceedings, food and drug regulation, interstate commerce, environmental laws, intellectual property, international trade, labor standards, maritime issues, securities, telecommunications, and so on. However, Puerto Rico differs from the states in terms of its local economic institutions. Specifically, areas such as business permits, contract law, mortgage law, professional regulation, real property transactions, and zoning reflect a strong influence from the Spanish civil law system.

downside of access to U.S. resources may be promotion of a culture of dependency.

Internally, the government's interactions with citizens and businesses lack transparency. Its tax policies are complex and inconsistent, and information on budget expenditures is difficult to obtain. In chapter 6, Steven J. Davis and Luis A. Rivera-Batiz observe that the regulatory system appears to be particularly complex and is a contributor to what is perceived as a difficult business environment. The balance of voting strength between the two main political parties has led to a focus on politics as opposed to economics and a lack of continuity in government economic policies. In addition, many current transfer programs are structured so as to provide disincentives for work. This issue is stressed by both Gary Burtless and Orlando Sotomayor in chapter 3 and by María E. Enchautegui and Richard B. Freeman in chapter 4. The U.S. minimum wage (currently $5.15 an hour) applies to Puerto Rico; but given wage rates that average only half those of the mainland, the minimum wage has a much larger constraining effect on job opportunities for lower-skilled workers. There is also evidence, presented by Helen F. Ladd and Francisco L. Rivera-Batiz in chapter 5, that the quality of a once enviable education system is deteriorating.

Legacy of the Past

In chapter 2, Barry P. Bosworth and Susan M. Collins have provided a detailed review of Puerto Rico's past growth performance. That analysis suggests a break in economic performance in the 1970s, with much lower rates of economic growth in succeeding decades. In that and later chapters on more specific aspects of the economy, the contributors to this volume have suggested that several changes in the economic environment and policies contributed to the slowdown. By the early 1970s the process of shifting workers out of low-productivity agriculture into industry and services was complete, and growth became more dependent on improving productivity within the major sectors. Most strikingly, the industrialization program known as Operation Bootstrap ran out of steam after 1970. It was always a program that relied heavily on large multinational companies headquartered on the mainland, and it did little to build links with local supplying firms. As a result, Puerto Rico did not develop a large cadre of dynamic local entrepreneurs like that which emerged in the East Asian economies, nor was there significant transfer of know-how from the multinationals to Puerto Rican firms.

Chapter 2 argues that the expansion of the section 936 tax program shifted the focus away from developing activities in which Puerto Rico had a comparative advantage toward those with significant tax advantages

to U.S. corporations. Growth was narrowly focused around a few manufacturing industries with large inputs of intangible capital (patents) that
benefited from Puerto Rico as a tax shelter. The narrowing of the base of
industrialization was also reflected in a sharp decline in capital investment during the 1980s.

The 1970s and early 1980s also witnessed a significant drop in rates
of labor force participation. Chapter 3 argues that the expansion of the
U.S. transfer programs in Puerto Rico during that period was a significant contributing factor to the decline in the participation rate. The level
of benefits provided by those programs was more attractive in Puerto
Rico, with its lower average wage rates, than in the United States.
As Burtless and Sotomayor show, there was a large increase in the proportion of Puerto Ricans receiving benefits from the various means-tested
programs in the 1970s and 1980s. The introduction of the U.S. minimum wage in Puerto Rico in the 1970s also played a role in reducing job
opportunities for the least educated portion of the population.

Today, Puerto Rico has an unusual industrial structure. As measured
by the distribution of employment, it has a very small private sector; and
within the private sector, the service-producing industries are underdeveloped. The missing jobs in Puerto Rico are largely in industries that would
employ the least educated workers. At the same time, Puerto Rico has not
generated growth in medium-sized enterprises, based locally, to offset the
declining role of the large mainland firms. In a variety of ways, such as occupational licensing and control of location decisions, the government has
restricted competition and the entry of new enterprises. The result is extensive rent-seeking behavior by those with links to the government. In several
respects, rather than fulfilling its earlier role of promoting innovative change,
the government of Puerto Rico has evolved over the years to become an
impediment to growth.

With the cancellation of the section 936 tax provisions, the relaxation of
U.S. trade barriers against other countries, and the emergence of numerous
other tax havens around the globe, Puerto Rico no longer has a significant
competitive advantage in the production of most manufacturing products
for the global market. In the area of pharmaceuticals, the buildup of a large
manufacturing infrastructure will continue to yield some advantages in
future years; but it is also a sector of rapid technological change in which
future manufacturing advantages are hard to predict.

However, Puerto Rico's economy is not in a state of collapse. The concern is that growth is insufficient to achieve progress in narrowing the
income differences between Puerto Rico and the U.S. mainland and that

poverty remains far too high. It also seems clear that the old strategy of attracting large offshore corporations has been exhausted. Puerto Rico needs a new approach to promoting convergence with mainland living standards.

Prescriptions for Restoring Growth

The preceding chapters present a number of policy actions that the authors believe have the potential to raise incomes in Puerto Rico. We will not repeat all of their suggestions; but we do identify five major policy areas that need to be addressed, and we discuss a number of specific policy proposals within each. The major issues are as follows:

—raising the employment rate of adult Puerto Ricans

—promoting a more dynamic private sector that would create additional job opportunities

—improving the skills of the workforce

—investing greater resources in the economic infrastructure

—reforming government with a more efficient tax system and targeted expenditure programs

Creating Employment

A large portion of the differences in income between Puerto Rico and the United States is the result of differences in the employment rate between the island and the mainland—that is, too few Puerto Ricans are actually working and earning income. The differences are particularly large for the least educated members of the population, but they remain substantial even for those with a tertiary level of education. If the employment rate of Puerto Rico could be increased to that of the mainland, while average wage rates were maintained, per capita income would rise by 50 percent.

The causes of the low employment rate among adults in Puerto Rico are not fully understood. In particular, not enough is known about the economic situation of individuals who report that they are not currently employed. Much could be learned if the monthly household employment survey were expanded on a temporary basis to ask more questions of individuals who report their status as out of the workforce. Why are they not seeking employment? Do health problems keep them from working? Do they believe that no job exists? Are they engaged in other activities?

Reaching the goal of parity with the employment rate of the mainland is a challenging but achievable task. Over the next quarter century, Puerto Rico

Table 10-2. *Employment Growth, Puerto Rico and Selected States and Countries, 1976–2001*[a]

Units as indicated

State or country	Employment in 2001 (thousands)	Average annual percent change, 1976–2001
Puerto Rico	1,136	2.4
United States	131,826	2.0
Arizona	2,265	4.5
Florida	7,171	3.9
Wisconsin (median state)	2,814	2.0
Korea	18,721	5.3
Ireland	1,533	4.6
Singapore	2,047	3.5

Source: Data for U.S. states from U.S Bureau of Labor Statistics, *Current Employment Survey,* various years; for Puerto Rico, Puerto Rico Planning Board; for Korea and Ireland, Organization for Economic Cooperation and Development; for Singapore, the International Labor Organization.

a. Data are for total nonfarm employment. Data for Korea are for 1972–97, and for Ireland, 1990–2000.

will experience a sharp deceleration of growth in the population of labor force age, to an average growth rate near zero. Over a twenty-five-year horizon, employment would need to grow by about 1.7 percent a year to raise Puerto Rico's labor force participation rate from its current 46 percent to the mainland average of 66 percent and to lower the unemployment rate from 10 percent to 6 percent of the labor force. If the goal were to be achieved over a fifteen-year period, employment growth would need to be 3 percent a year. As shown in table 10-2, employment grew at a 2.4 percent rate in Puerto Rico over the last twenty-five years of the century, and growth rates in excess of 3 percent were achieved in fast-growing regions of the United States as well as in countries such as Ireland, Korea, and Singapore. Admittedly, these growth rates benefited from rapid growth in the underlying population, but they suggest that the proposed target for employment growth is feasible.

The current low employment rate reflects long-standing problems on both the supply side, in terms of incentives to seek employment, and the demand side, in the form of limited job opportunities. Specifically, as argued by the authors of both chapter 3 and chapter 4, the design of the public transfer system in Puerto Rico discourages work effort. These disincentives are magnified for those with the lowest expected earnings: the young, the old, and those with the least education. The structures of the transfer programs, with the emphasis on means-testing of benefits, results in a situation in which many families would receive little additional net income if one more adult member obtained a job. Means-tested programs also have work-disincentive effects on the mainland. But these effects are considerably more problematic in Puerto Rico, where they influence a much larger proportion of the working population.

Puerto Rico needs to reform its social protection programs to promote efforts by individuals to seek employment. Enactment of an earned income tax credit, similar to that available on the mainland, is one reform that has been proposed for the island.[4] Unlike transfer programs whose benefit level declines as an individual's earnings rise, the earned income tax credit rises in step with earnings up to a ceiling amount. Beyond the ceiling, the credit is gradually phased out. It is a proven effective program that has been used to assist low-income working families on the mainland. The program should be financed by scaling back the benefits paid under other transfer programs, such as the Nutritional Assistance Program, that currently impose no work requirement.

Other transfer programs that are administered by the commonwealth government should also be reviewed with the objective of maximizing incentives to maintain employment. Puerto Rico operates an extensive social safety net, with public provision of housing, food, and medical care assistance. It needs to make access to that assistance network conditional on employment or strong efforts to obtain employment and to limit the duration of benefits that are not linked to employment.

The Social Security retirement program is administered by the federal government, and its rules cannot and should not be modified to the special circumstances of Puerto Rico, since it is vital that workers remain free to move between the island and the mainland without complication. However, as highlighted in chapters 3 and 4, rates of disability are much higher in Puerto Rico than on the mainland. It would be appropriate for the Social Security Administration to review this experience to ensure its consistency with overall program requirements.

In addition, Puerto Rico needs to follow the lead of many U.S. states in developing a network of training and education programs to meet the occupational education needs of potential labor force entrants into the local economy.[5] Workforce development programs combine secondary vocational training, community colleges, welfare-to-work programs, regional development agencies, and employer organizations to provide a full range of training and related employment services. An integrated approach helps increase employers' access to a skilled workforce and helps individuals to find career

4. Enchautegui (2003).
5. Puerto Rico has introduced some elements of a workforce development program with its Council on Human Resources and Occupational Development.

jobs. It also ensures that the educational system is responsive to changing labor market conditions; it goes beyond learning to assist in preparing individuals to enter or reenter the labor market.[6]

Private Sector Development

We believe that much of the problem of too few individuals working originates on the demand side of the market in the form of limited job opportunities. This aspect is stressed in chapter 6 of this volume. Measured by jobs, Puerto Rico has a very small private business sector. In its pursuit of large multinational corporations from the mainland, the Puerto Rican government has stifled the development of the local business economy and discouraged the development of linkages between foreign-based and local firms that normally makes the pursuit of foreign direct investment a desirable part of a progrowth strategy. For example, because the government imposed local employment quotas on the multinationals, the companies were unwilling to outsource even the simplest of support services, an important channel through which local firms in other countries learn from the multinationals.

There is no simple answer to the problem of an underdeveloped local business sector because the factors that contribute to it are deeply embedded in an overly complex tax system, a stifling regulatory regime, and a political process that is heavily dominated by competing rent-seeking interest groups. In past years, the government has initiated numerous economic development programs; but follow-up efforts have been unfocused, and the programs are often cast aside with the next shift of administration.

Puerto Rico needs to create and sustain a comprehensive program to promote the development of island-based businesses that can provide the job opportunities that are currently lacking. That effort will require a greater focus on small and medium-sized enterprises, and it should be coordinated by a government agency dedicated to promoting the interests of those firms. The program should address five major problem areas by eliminating excessive regulatory burdens, ensuring access to financial capital, improving training for entrepreneurs and their employees, increasing access to the research and development network, and developing core business areas of sufficient size to generate significant synergies.

---

6. Robert Giloth (1998) provides a range of perspectives on workforce development programs with case studies. A wide range of information on the role of community colleges is available at the website of the Community College Research Center, Columbia University (ccrc.tc.columbia.edu/Home.asp [February 2006]).

Davis and Luis Rivera-Batiz emphasize the importance of reforming the regulatory environment surrounding the entry of new business firms and their development. Previous attempts to change an administrative regime that is viewed as inhospitable to business, however, have met with limited success. Efforts have been made to transfer the permitting process to municipalities and grant them greater authority to institute reforms. However, as the authors point out, this is not a practical solution for an economy comprising seventy-eight municipalities. Reform needs to be concentrated at the commonwealth level with the elimination of unneeded regulations and licensing requirements that suppress new business and the streamlining of the permit process in a single, one-stop coordinating office.

Financing is always a problem for small and medium-sized companies. However, it is not evident that it is the major barrier in Puerto Rico. Enterprises on the island are eligible for the loan guarantee and other support programs of the federal Small Business Administration. The agency operates a district office in Puerto Rico, and local firms appear to be active participants in the loan guarantee program, according to data for fiscal year 2005. The volume of loans ($163 million), scaled by personal income, is above the national average and even above fast-growing states such as Florida. Arguments are made, however, that new firms do not have the benefit of a program of active support from venture capitalists and peer-to-peer networks that can assist start-up firms. As noted in chapter 8, twelve venture capital funds are known to operate in Puerto Rico, but the amount of funding appears to be low. It is difficult to determine whether this lack of funding of innovative business activities represents a financing problem or is a reflection of limited entrepreneurial activity.

Puerto Rican firms are also eligible for the Small Business Innovative Research program, which reserves a small portion of federal R&D grants for small business. The program funds the critical start-up and development stages, and it encourages the commercialization of new technologies, products, and services. While Puerto Rican firms have received such grants, the magnitude of the grants between 2000 and 2004 has been very small. Over the period, Puerto Rico ranks below all the U.S. states both in terms of total dollar amount of such grants and in total amount of grants as a percentage of total personal income.[7]

Within Puerto Rico, the need to improve educational programs in the area of business and entrepreneurial skills is often mentioned as a barrier

7. Data on grant activity by state are available from the Small Business Administration (www.sba.gov/sbir/indexsbir-sttr.html [February 2006]).

to the growth of local businesses. For example, the government's recent visioning exercise, "Puerto Rico 2025," emphasizes the need to strengthen business training, promote a closer link between the universities and the local business community, and encourage the formation of business networks among local small and medium-sized enterprises. Such activities are also closely related to the expansion of workforce development programs discussed in the prior section.

While R&D and linkages between the research institutions and local business are often mentioned as a priority for economic development in Puerto Rico, the available data suggest it is currently an area of considerable weakness. As noted earlier, Puerto Rico is underrepresented in the federal Small Business Innovative Research program. In addition, the island ranks below all the U.S. states as a recipient of federal research funds and in the category of academic R&D expenditures, even when the measures are scaled by personal income of the state.[8] Furthermore, the number of scientists and engineers as a percentage of the labor force is below that of the states. Puerto Rico has much to do to build a significant R&D base for future economic activities.

In chapter 9, on trade and industrial policy, Robert Z. Lawrence and Juan Lara suggest that Puerto Rico should focus on a development strategy that concentrates on a few industrial clusters, such as pharmaceuticals manufacturing, in which Puerto Rico might expect to develop a strong comparative advantage. The concept emphasizes linkages among private firms, research centers, and government agencies. It is similar to the approach adopted by the Puerto Rico Industrial Development Company. But at present, research and development is not a high priority within the university system, and few private firms are engaged in such activities. Thus the government would have to do much more than at present to fund a local research program.[9] In addition, the list developed by the Puerto Rico Industrial Development Company is too extensive for an economy of Puerto Rico's size.

Puerto Rico is likely to do better as a regional center for finance and business services. It is well located relative to the United States, Latin America, and Europe. It has a strong banking sector and a pool of bilingual educated labor to work in key areas of business services. It also has a fairly strong base

8. Data from National Science Foundation, Division of Science Resources Statistics, *Science and Engineering State Profiles, 2001–2003,* 2005 (www.nsf.gov/statistics/nsf05301/ [February 2006]). Information could not be obtained on the magnitude of industry R&D in Puerto Rico.

9. Actions were taken in 2005 to begin construction of a biotechnology center under the sponsorship of the University of Puerto Rico and the Puerto Rico Industrial Development Company.

in information and communications technologies. At present, however, most professional service firms are small, with a limited amount of activity outside of Puerto Rico. Thus the island would need to expend considerable effort to promote the sector and improve the underlying infrastructure. There is much to learn from the related experience of Singapore as a business center in Southeast Asia, and Ireland's development of business links with the rest of Europe.

U.S. regulations handicapped Puerto Rico in any effort to become a business logistics center. Nearly all goods trade between the island and the mainland is subject to the Jones Act, which requires that the goods move in U.S.-built, U.S.-owned, and U.S.-manned ships. This constitutes a significant cost barrier for Puerto Rico as it competes with Mexico, which has equivalent access to the U.S. markets under the North American Free Trade Agreement but is not subject to the provisions of the Jones Act. The issue will take on increased importance with implementation of the Central American Free Trade Agreement, which will further isolate Puerto Rico. Furthermore, Puerto Rico is considered to be part of the United States for purposes of international agreements on air transport, restricting travel between the United States and Puerto Rico to U.S.-flagged airlines. As a result of these measures, Puerto Rico's ability to act as a transportation hub serving the United States, Latin America, and the rest of the world is constrained. The United States could assist the island's development as a regional business center by exempting it from these transportation restrictions.

Finally, actions should be taken to act the application of the minimum wage in Puerto Rico. Under pressure from U.S. trade unions looking to restrict competition with the mainland, the federal minimum wage was imposed on Puerto Rico in the 1970s. Because prevailing wages are only half those of the mainland, however, the U.S. minimum on the island constitutes a far larger barrier to the employment of low-skilled workers than in the states. The current U.S. minimum of $5.15 is equivalent to a $10.00 minimum wage on the mainland. According to the 2000 census, 37 percent of Puerto Rican workers report hourly earnings of less than $6.00, compared with only 14 percent on the mainland. While the minimum wage may raise the earnings of some workers, it eliminates job opportunities for low-skilled workers. Employers will not hire workers whose productivity is less than the minimum wage. The system is particularly constraining on the employment of young first-time entrants to the job market. Puerto Rico needs to regain the right to impose minimum wage rates in line with its own prevailing wage structure.

Education Reform

A dramatic gain in educational attainment stands out as a major contributor to Puerto Rico's past economic growth. However, as highlighted by Ladd and Rivera-Batiz, there is evidence that this area of former strength is now encountering significant problems. Families that can afford to do so are abandoning the public school system in response to problems of violence, perceptions of declining quality, and a lack of accountability at all levels. These problems are similar to those faced by many large urban systems on the mainland, but the rate of deterioration seems more rapid in Puerto Rico.

Like all U.S. states, Puerto Rico is subject to the test-based accountability provisions of the federal No Child Left Behind Act of 2001. The provisions of the act can be useful in developing meaningful measures of performance and in establishing stronger accountability standards. The test-based assessments can help guide the reallocation of education resources to the areas of greatest need. In strengthening accountability, Ladd and Rivera-Batiz also suggest, Puerto Rico can learn from the experience of mainland school systems, such as Chicago, that faced similar problems but have made progress in recent years. Given the failure of the education reform efforts of the 1990s and a highly politicized education system, Puerto Rico may have to consider some of the extreme management changes that were made in Chicago.

Puerto Rico faces different problems within its system of higher education. Both the proportion of the population aged eighteen to twenty-four that is enrolled and the proportion of enrollees who receive a degree are similar to the U.S. average; but there are concerns about the quality of the education. For example, the proportion of students receiving graduate degrees is low, faculty salaries are low, and research and development activity is limited. The cost per student in the public system is again similar to the U.S. average; but the proportion paid for by tuition is far below that in the United States, and the system's dependency on public funds is far greater. In effect, Puerto Ricans pay a much larger proportion of their taxes to subsidize the university system, with no evidence of comparable returns.

The result, as Ladd and Rivera-Batiz point out, is a substantial public subsidy to high-income families, who are more likely to have a member attending the university. A more efficient system would use public funds to provide financial assistance, in the form of grants and loans, directly to students and let them chose among the available institutions. The result would be greater competition among the higher-education institutions to provide a quality education. At the same time, more needs to be done to promote

R&D activities and interactions between the institutions and the local economy. In effect, Puerto Rico needs to use its university system to strengthen its comparative advantage in knowledge-based industries and to promote its efforts to become a regional center for business services.

The Physical Infrastructure

The quality of Puerto Rico's physical infrastructure needs to be improved. As documented in chapter 2, on growth performance, the island suffers from a congested road system, inefficient provision of electrical energy, and a communications system that lags behind that of the mainland. Overall, the quality of the infrastructure is superior to that of most industrializing countries, but it falls short of the higher-income countries with which Puerto Rico is trying to compete.

The need for reform is most urgent in the area of electric energy. The high cost of energy is a significant barrier to the expansion of the island's industrial base. As documented by Sergio Marxuach, the cost of electric power is far above that on the mainland, and the Puerto Rico Electric Power Authority is highly inefficient relative to other comparable utilities.[10] The government should begin immediately to restructure this public enterprise, with the ultimate objective of increasing the availability of high-quality, reliable, and cost-efficient electric power in Puerto Rico. In addition, an independent regulatory board should be created to provide oversight of both the generation and distribution of electricity. Exposure to the international energy market is high, however, as the island has few internal sources.

The Puerto Rico Telephone Company has been effectively privatized. Verizon Corporation holds a controlling interest, and the government is a minority stockholder. Despite substantial investment in recent years, Puerto Rico lags behind other advanced economies in many dimensions of communications use. In part, the low usage, as measured by indicators such as the number of Internet connections, can be explained by the current industrial mix; but if Puerto Rico hopes to become an important regional center for business services, it will need a superior communications system. A study aimed at accounting for the low usage of information and communications technologies would have considerable value.

In addition, Puerto Rico needs to improve the quality of what are at present deteriorating transportation and water and sewer systems. These are all areas of importance in expanding the island's economy and improving the quality of life; but they will require better management and substantial

10. Marxuach (2005).

Figure 10-1. *General Fund Revenues and Expenditures as Share of Gross National Income, Puerto Rico, 1990–2004*

Percent of GNI

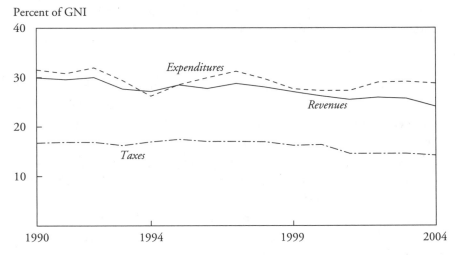

Source: Data are from Puerto Rico Department of Treasury (1990–2004), "Statistical section."

public investment. Given the government's fiscal problems, it is imperative that these efforts be financed by greater reliance on user fees.

Government Reform

The government of Puerto Rico is faced with growing fiscal problems. In recent years it has experienced substantial budget deficits that would be even larger were it not for the use of nonrecurring income and other temporary actions to cover the shortfalls. The public debt is rising as a proportion of income, and the government is faced with a large unfunded liability in its employee pension system. These problems, together with the lack of a plan to deal with them, have resulted in a deteriorating bond rating that by 2005 was at the lowest investment grade.

The general trends in Puerto Rican revenues and expenditures are shown in figure 10-1. Expenditures as a share of the island's income have been slowly declining in recent years; but the decline in revenues has been even more rapid, owing largely to the erosion of the tax base. Federal government payments are also a major revenue source, about 30 percent of the total (not shown).

As James Alm reports in chapter 7, the size and composition of government expenditures in the major program areas is similar to that of the U.S. states. It is difficult to make a detailed comparison because of the greater importance of government enterprises that operate outside of the General

Fund. Some enterprises supply services that are often provided by the private sector in the United States, but others represent activities that would normally be classified as government activities.[11] Moreover, it matters greatly whether the comparison is based on gross domestic product (income produced in Puerto Rico) or gross national income (the net income of residents). According to Alm, U.S. state and local taxes have averaged about9 percent of gross state product in recent years. In Puerto Rico, taxes are a similar share of gross domestic product but a larger 14 percent share of gross national income.[12] On an employment basis, public administration is 30 percent of nonagricultural employment, compared with 14 percent in the states.[13]

Puerto Rico has an extraordinarily complex tax system, as Alm notes, with numerous layers of conflicting tax preferences. The problems are particularly severe with the taxation of business activities. The commonwealth imposes a hefty tax on corporate income, with rates rising to 39 percent, but it exempts large numbers of both domestic and foreign-based firms from the tax. Many of these exemptions are negotiated between individual corporations and the government, with effective tax rates as low as zero. In today's global economy, the taxation of business activities at rates above those of competitive locations can easily lead to a diversion of business, particularly of those businesses aimed at the export market. However, Puerto Rico's current approach of negotiating special deals with foreign-based corporations can easily disadvantage its own Puerto Rican businesses.

The individual income tax has also accumulated a significant number of special provisions and exemptions that have eroded the effective tax base. With exemptions for many forms of capital income and under-reporting of self-employment income, the tax is largely a wage tax. Despite a range of marginal tax rates from 7 to 38 percent, the effective tax on total personal income is less than 6 percent. Such a large difference between

11. Examples of enterprises that operate outside the governmental funds are the Puerto Rico Electric Power Authority, the Government Development Bank, and the University of Puerto Rico. We have focused on the governmental funds, which report only the net payments to government enterprises (excluding their other sources of revenue).

12. Puerto Rico does not regularly publish aggregate data on the tax revenues of municipal governments, but they are less significant than in the average state. Employment in the municipalities is about 20 percent of total public administration, compared with more than 60 percent in the states. Revenues are obtained from a property tax, construction fees, and transfers from the central government.

13. Again, however, it is important to remember that the share of the population working in public administration is much more similar to that in the United States. As noted in several prior chapters, Puerto Rico has a very low employment-to-population ratio.

average and marginal rates implies the potential for major tax distortions. Puerto Rico also imposes a number of excise taxes and a sales tax on manufactures and imports.

There is a growing recognition of the need to reform the tax system, but a consensus on the characteristics of the new system has not emerged. We would suggest, first, that attention be paid to the importance of combining a broad tax base with low rates, as the available tax research highlights. High tax rates are the primary cause of the economic distortions and incentives to evade the tax. Second, in a highly competitive global economy, Puerto Rico needs to be made an attractive base for international business. That calls for a simple and highly transparent system of business taxation with low rates. Third, Puerto Rico could reduce many of it problems with tax evasion and disincentives toward work by placing greater reliance on a broad-based consumption tax. Fourth, Puerto Rico needs to reform what has become an absurd system of property taxation.

In the past, Puerto Rico could rely on its special appeal for U.S. corporations who took advantage of section 936 of the U.S. tax code. But with the elimination of that provision and the conversion of U.S. subsidiaries to controlled foreign corporations (CFCs), Puerto Rico must compete with other countries as a base for those CFCs engaged in export-based production. It can no longer maintain a system of cross-subsidization in which large business taxes support subsidies to the resident population.

As Alm observes, many of the problems of the current tax regime could be reduced by shifting to a greater emphasis on a broad-based consumption tax. There are basically two alternatives: a retail sales tax, such as that used in the U.S. states, or a value added tax (VAT). We believe that in the case of Puerto Rico, there are clear advantages to the VAT. The retail sales tax is employed in the United States largely because the individual states do not have information on the volume of cross-border transactions.[14] A VAT generally imposes the tax on imports and rebates it on exports. However, as an island economy, Puerto Rico can easily introduce such a system for transborder transactions. Second, Puerto Rico is said to have a severe problem with tax avoidance and a growing underground economy. Those problems are aggravated by the retail sales tax but minimized under a VAT. If an enterprise does not pay the tax on its sales, it cannot deduct the tax paid on its purchased inputs. Each firm has an incentive to ensure that its sup-

14. The retail sales tax is also encountering increased problems with the growth of Internet sales. There have been ongoing discussions of a national VAT, with a state allocation of the proceeds on the basis of state income or population, but it is hard to reach any agreement among such a large group of diverse interests.

pliers have paid the tax in order to claim it as a credit. The VAT has been the overwhelming choice of countries that have enacted consumption-based tax regimes.

A broad-based consumption tax will fall more heavily on low-income households because they spend a larger portion of their income in the local economy. However, efforts to deal with that problem by exempting some items, such as food and medicine, are quite ineffective because the exemptions are not closely correlated with income, and the special provisions greatly complicate the tax system. It is more effective to focus instead on the distributional concerns in designing the income tax system, which can be tailored more closely to the economic situation of individuals and can easily be made more progressive as an offset to a regressive consumption tax.

The continued reliance on 1958 property values in the determination of property tax assessments makes no sense. A rational system of property taxation is an important means of diversifying the government's revenue base, and the tax helps ensure the efficient use of a valuable resource. Ideally, the tax should apply only to the value of the underlying land so as not to discourage improvements in the accompanying structures, but the assessment of land independently of the structure is a difficult undertaking. A property tax also works best when the total amount of the tax is maintained at a relatively modest level.

The problems of the government sector, however, go beyond a need for reform of the tax system. The operations of the government lack transparency, with far too great a reliance on special administrative, tax, and regulatory actions tailored to the interests of individual groups. Like many states, Puerto Rico has a constitutional requirement for a balanced budget, but the requirement is consistently circumvented by reliance on short-term borrowing from the Government Development Bank or other funds or by reliance on one-time revenue inflows. The lack of fiscal discipline has created a serious threat that Puerto Rico could lose its access to debt markets.

Concluding Thoughts

Puerto Rico has made many impressive economic achievements, and its citizens enjoy a standard of living above that of any economy of Latin America. Yet, equally relevant, it is poorer than the poorest American state by a substantial margin, and more than half of its children live below the U.S. poverty line. Furthermore, the narrowing of the income gap between Puerto Rico and the mainland has stalled. In this chapter we examined the economic issues from the perspective that Puerto Rico can and should do better. We have argued that its highly skilled population and its physical and social infrastructure provide the requisite base from which to launch rapid economic growth in future years. Persistence of the currently high rates of poverty should be unacceptable—both to Puerto Rican residents and to their fellow citizens on the mainland.

Participants in the project on which this volume was based uncovered a fascinating set of economic puzzles in struggling to understand why Puerto Rico's economic growth faltered recently, despite strong performance before the 1970s. Why does the income gap with the mainland persist in the presence of a common set of economic, legal, and social institutions and a population that has made such remarkable strides in educational attainment? The chapters in this volume, we believe, offer insights that can account for key dimensions of Puerto Rico's economic performance. They also outline a set of proposals that we think would help restore higher rates of economic growth and improve the standard of living relative to that of the mainland.

However, we would be remiss if we did not emphasize that Puerto Rico is at an important crossroads as it seeks to develop and implement a strategy for future growth. Evolution of the global economy and developments within its own region dictate that the policies it pursued in the past will not work for the future. Puerto Rico cannot continue to rely on tax advantages as the primary attraction for multinational firms. Instead, Puerto Rico must diversify and strengthen its economy by developing its own dynamic private businesses and the jobs that they will bring.

References

Alesina, Alberto, and Edward L. Glaeser. 2004. *Fighting Poverty in the U.S. and Europe: A World of Difference.* Oxford University Press.

Alm, James, and Janet L. Rogers. 2005. "Do State Fiscal Policies Affect Economic Growth?" Working Paper. Andrew Young School of Policy Studies, Georgia State University.

Baumol, William, and Edward N. Wolff. 1996. "Catching up in the Postwar Period: Puerto Rico as the Fifth Tiger." *World Development* 24 (5): 869–85.

Bosworth, Barry, and Susan M. Collins. 2003. "The Empirics of Growth: An Update." *Brookings Papers on Economic Activity 2:* 113–206.

Bosworth, Barry P., and Susan M. Collins. 2006. "Economic Growth." In *The Economy of Puerto Rico: Restoring Growth,* edited by Susan M. Collins, Barry P. Bosworth, and Miguel A. Soto-Class. Center for the New Economy and Brookings.

Cao García, Ramón J. 2004. *Impuestos en Puerto Rico: Treinta Años de Experiencias y Estudios.* San Juan.

Castillo-Freeman, Alida, and Richard Freeman. 1992. "When the Minimum Wage Really Bites: The Effect of the U.S.-Level Minimum on Puerto Rico." In *Immigration and the Work Force,* edited by George Borjas and Richard Freeman, pp. 177–212. University of Chicago Press.

———. 1991. "Minimum Wages in Puerto Rico: Textbook Case of a Wage Floor?" Working Paper 3759. Cambridge, Mass.: National Bureau of Economic Research.

Castillo Ortiz, Alicia, and Glory Marrero. 2003. "Study of Absenteeism among Teachers and Students in the Public Schools of Puerto Rico." University of Puerto Rico, Graduate School of Education.

Collins, Susan M., Barry P. Bosworth, and Miguel A. Soto-Class., eds. 2006. *The Economy of Puerto Rico: Restoring Growth.* Center for the New Economy and Brookings.

Commonwealth of Puerto Rico. 1994. *Budget of the Commonwealth of Puerto Rico.* San Juan: Office of Management and Budget of Puerto Rico.

_____. 1996. *Budget of the Commonwealth of Puerto Rico.* San Juan: Office of Management and Budget of Puerto Rico.

_____. 1998. *Budget of the Commonwealth of Puerto Rico.* San Juan: Office of Management and Budget of Puerto Rico.

_____. 2000. *Budget of the Commonwealth of Puerto Rico.* San Juan: Office of Management and Budget of Puerto Rico.

———. 2003. "Rethinking Our Department of Education: Transition Report." San Juan: Department of Education.

_____. 2004a. *Budget of the Commonwealth of Puerto Rico.* San Juan: Office of Management and Budget of Puerto Rico.

———. 2004b. "Rethinking Our Department of Education: Proposed Model." San Juan: Department of Education.

Contos, George, and Ellen Legel. 2000. "Corporation Income Tax Returns, 1997." *Statistics of Income Bulletin* (Summer): 101–21 (www.irs.gov/taxstats/article/0,,id=96388,00.html [August 2004]).

Corneo, Giacomo, and Hans Peter Gruener. 2002. "Individual Preferences for Political Redistribution." *Journal of Public Economics* 83 (1): 83–107.

Dietz, James. 2002. "Puerto Rico: The Three-Legged Economy." *Integration and Trade* 5(15): 247–73.

———. 2003. *Puerto Rico: Negotiating Development and Change.* Boulder, Colo.: Lynne Rienner.

Dunn, Thomas A., and Douglas J. Holtz-Eakin. 2000. "Financial Capital, Human Capital, and the Transition to Self-Employment: Evidence from Intergenerational Links." *Journal of Labor Economics* 18, no. 2: 282–305.

Enchautegui, María E. 2003. *Reaping the Benefits of Work: A Tax Credit for Low-Income Working Families in Puerto Rico.* San Juan: Center for the New Economy (www.grupocne.org/ [February 2006]).

Estado Libre Asociado de Puerto Rico. 2002. *Serie histórica de empleo y desempleo: Años naturales, 1970–2001.* San Juan: Departamento del Trabajo y Recursos Humanos, Negociado de Estadísticas.

Estudios Técnicos. 2003. "The Study of Economic Development in Puerto Rico: Summaries of Major Contributions." Mimeo.

———. 2004. *La economía informal en Puerto Rico: Primo, segundo, y tercer informe.* Report prepared by Estudios Técnicos for the Department of Labor and Human Resources. San Juan (October).

Fairlie, Robert W., and Alicia Robb. 2003. "Families, Human Capital, and Small Business: Evidence from the Characteristics of Business Owners Survey." Economic Growth Center Discussion Paper 871. Yale University.

Freeman, Richard B., and Maria E. Enchautegui. 2006. "Why Don't More Puerto Rican Men Work? The Rich Uncle (Sam) Hypothesis." In *The Economy of Puerto Rico: Restoring Growth,* edited by Susan M. Collins, Barry P. Bosworth, and Miguel A. Soto-Class. Center for the New Economy and Brookings.

Freeman, Richard B., and Remco Oostendorp. 2002. "Wages around the World: Pay across Occupations and Countries." In *Inequality around the World,* edited by Richard B. Freeman. London: Palgrave.

Gillis, Malcolm. 1985. "Micro and Macroeconomics of Tax Reform in Indonesia." *Journal of Development Economics* 19(3): 221–254.

Gregg, Paul, and Jonathan Wadsworth. 2001. "Everything You Ever Wanted to Know about Measuring Worklessness and Polarization at the Household Level but Were Afraid to Ask." *Oxford Bulletin of Economics and Statistics* 63, no. S1 (September).

Giloth, Robert P., ed. 1998. *Jobs and Economic Development: Strategies and Practice.* Thousand Oaks, Calif.: Sage Publications.

Grubert, Harry, and Joel Slemrod. 1998. "The Effect of Taxes on Investment and Income Shifting to Puerto Rico." *Review of Economics and Statistics* 80, no. 3: 365–73.

Hausmann, Ricardo, Lant Pritchett, and Dani Rodrik. 2004. "Growth Accelerations." Working Paper 10566. Cambridge, Mass.: National Bureau of Economic Research (June).

Hausmann, Ricardo, and Dani Rodrik. 2003. "Economic Development as Self-Discovery." *Journal of Development Economics* 72, no. 2: 603–33.

Hout, Michael, and Harvey S. Rosen. 2000. "Self-Employment, Family Background, and Race." *Journal of Human Resources* 35, no. 4: 670–92.

Jacobson, Louis, Robert J. LaLonde, and Daniel G. Sullivan. 1993. "Earnings Losses of Displaced Workers." *American Economic Review* 83, no. 4 (September): 685–709.

Katz, Lawrence F., and David H. Autor. 1999. "Changes in the Wage Structure and Earnings Inequality." In *Handbook of Labor Economics,* vol. 3A, edited by Orley Ashenfelter and David Card. Amsterdam: North Holland.

Krueger, Alan. 1995. "The Effect of the Minimum Wage When It Really Bites: A Reexamination of the Evidence from Puerto Rico." In *Research in Labor Economics,* vol. 14, edited by Solomon Polachek. Greenwich, Conn.: JAI Press.

Kaufmann, Daniel, Aart Kraay, and Pablo Zoido-Lobatón. 2002. "Governance Matters II: Updated Indicators for 2000–01." Policy Research Working Paper 2772. Washington: World Bank.

Marxuach, Sergio M. 2005. "Restructuring the Puerto Rico Electricity Sector." White Paper 3. San Juan: Center for the New Economy (August 11).

Moody's Investors Service, Global Credit Research. 2005. "Moody's Downgrades Commonwealth of Puerto Rico's G.O. Bonds to Baa2." Special Comment (May).

National Center for Education Statistics. 2003. *Digest of Education Statistics 2002.* Washington: U.S. Department of Education.

———. 2004. *Digest of Education Statistics 2003.* Washington: U.S. Department of Education.

National Science Foundation, Division of Science Resources Statistics. 2005. *Science and Engineering State Profiles, 2001-03.* (The 2001-03 report is available at www.nsf.gov/statistics/nsf05301/.)

Neal, Derek. 1995. "Industry-Specific Human Capital: Evidence from Displaced Workers." *Journal of Labor Economics* 13, no. 4 (October): 653–77.

Padin, Jose A. 2003. "Puerto Rico in the Post War: Liberalized Development Banking and the Fall of the 'Fifth Tiger.'" *World Development* 31, no. 2: 281–301.

Pantojas-Garcia, Emilio. 1999. "Los estudios económicos sobre Puerto Rico: Una evaluación critica." In *El futuro económico de Puerto Rico,* edited by Francisco Martinez, pp. 11–26. San Juan: Editorial de la Universidad de Puerto Rico.

Parent, Daniel. 2000. "Industry-Specific Capital and the Wage Profile: Evidence from the National Longitudinal Survey of Youth and the Panel Study of Income Dynamics." *Journal of Labor Economics* 18, no. 2: 306–21.

Pavcnik, Nina. 2003. "What Explains Skill Upgrading in Less Developed Countries?" *Journal of Development Economics* 71, no. 2: 311–28.

Planning Board, Office of the Governor, Commonwealth of Puerto Rico. 2003a. *Income and Product 2003 (Ingreso y Producto).*

————. 2003b. "Statistical Appendix." *Economic Report to the Governor, 2003 (Informe Económico a la Gobernado).*

————. 2004. "Statistical Appendix." *Economic Report to the Governor, 2004 (Informe Económico a la Gobernado).*

Pol, Julio Cesar. 2004. "Estimaciones de la economía subterránea: El caso de Puerto Rico." *Ensayos y Monografías* 117. San Juan: Universidad de Puerto Rico, Unidad de Investigaciones Económicas.

Puerto Rico Department of Treasury. 1990–2004. *Comprehensive Annual Financial Report,* annual reports (www.hacienda.gobierno.pr/estados_fin/index.html [April 2006]).

Rivera-Batiz, Francisco. 1993. *Study of the Budget of the Department of Education of Puerto Rico.* San Juan: General Council of Education.

————. 2003. "The Impact of School-to-Work Programs on Minority Youth." In *The School-to-Work Movement: Origins and Destinations,* edited by William J. Stull and Nicholas M. Sanders, pp. 169–88. Westport, Conn.: Praeger.

Rivera-Batiz, Francisco, and Carlos Santiago. 1996. *Island Paradox: Puerto Rico in the 1990s.* New York: Russell Sage Foundation.

Rodrik, Dani. 2004. "Industrial Policy for the Twenty-First Century." Paper prepared for UNIDO, September.

Ruggles, Steven, and others. 2004. *Integrated Public Use Microdata Series: Version 3.* Minneapolis: Minnesota Population Center (www.ipums.org).

Schneider, Friedrich, and Dominik H. Enste. 2002. *The Shadow Economy—An International Survey.* Cambridge University Press.

Sotomayor, Orlando. 2004. "Development and Income Distribution: The Case of Puerto Rico." *World Development* 32, no. 8: 1395–406.

Standard & Poor's. 2005. "Puerto Rico's GO Debt Rating Lowered to 'BBB'; Growing Structural Imbalance Cited" (May 24).

Toledo, Wilfredo, and Wilfredo Camacho. 1997. *Análisis de opiniones y percepciones de los contribuyentes sobre la labor del Departmento de Hacienda.* San Juan: Statistics and Economics Consulting Group.

United Nations, Economic Commission for Latin American and the Caribbean. 2004. *Globalización y Desarrollo: Desafíos de Puerto Rico Frente al Siglo XXI,* draft (December).

U.S. Department of Commerce. 2003. *U.S. Census of Population and Housing, 5% Public Use Microdata Samples.* Washington: Bureau of the Census.

University of Puerto Rico at Río Piedras. 2005. *Self-Study Report to the Middle States Commission on Higher Education.*

Contributors

JAMES ALM
Georgia State University

FUAT ANDIC
United Nations Adviser

MARINÉS APONTE
University of Puerto Rico

DAVID AUDRETSCH
Indiana University

WILLIAM BAUMOL
New York University

BARRY P. BOSWORTH
Brookings Institution

GARY BURTLESS
Brookings Institution

SUSAN M. COLLINS
*Brookings Institution and
    Georgetown University*

STEVEN J. DAVIS
University of Chicago

JAMES DIETZ
University of California–Fullerton

MARÍA E. ENCHAUTEGUI
University of Puerto Rico

ARTURO ESTRELLA
Federal Reserve Bank, New York

RONALD FISHER
Michigan State University

RICHARD B. FREEMAN
Harvard University

JAMES HANSON
World Bank

ALAN KRUEGER
Princeton University

HELEN F. LADD
Duke University

JUAN LARA
University of Puerto Rico

ROBERT Z. LAWRENCE
Harvard University

DANIEL LEDERMAN
World Bank

WILLIAM LOCKWOOD BENET
*Lockwood Financial Advisors and
   Generans Bioventures*

RITA MALDONADO-BEAR
New York University

BELINDA REYES
University of California–Merced

FRANCISCO L. RIVERA-BATIZ
Columbia University

LUIS A. RIVERA-BATIZ
University of Puerto Rico

CARLOS SANTIAGO
University of Wisconsin

EILEEN SEGARRA
University of Puerto Rico

MIGUEL A. SOTO-CLASS
Center for the New Economy

ORLANDO SOTOMAYOR
University of Puerto Rico

KATHERINE TERRELL
University of Michigan

JOSÉ JOAQUÍN VILLAMIL
University of Puerto Rico

INGO WALTER
New York University

Index

Administracion de Fomento Económico. *See* Industrial Development Company

AFICA. *See* Puerto Rico Industrial, Tourist, Educational, Medical, and Environmental Control Financing Authority

Agriculture, 11–12

Alm, James, 65–77, 120–21

Andic, Fuat, 76, 77

Andretsch, David, 63

Aponte, Marinés, 63

Argentina, 32, 44, 47

Asia, 5. *See also* East Asia; Southeast Asia

Autonomous Municipalities Law (*1991*; PR), 62

Banks and banking, 80–83, 86–88, 89, 116. *See also* Economic Development Bank; Government Development Bank

Baumol, William, 17

Bosworth, Barry P., 1–4, 5–17, 103–24

Burtless, Gary, 19–29, 110, 112

Business and corporate issues—Puerto Rico: business ownership, 57; climate for business development and employment growth, 55–63, 109, 110, 114; commer-cial and industrial loans, 80–81, 87–88; commercial banks, 81–82; education and training, 115; export promotion agency, 100; free enterprise segment, 57–58; Government Development Bank, 84–85; income shifting, 8; industry structure and human capital mix, 58–59; invest-ment, 11; local business sector, 114, 116–17; multinational corporations, 109, 114; permitting process, 62, 63, 115; privatization, 76, 119; reforms and recommendations, 62–63, 115–17; regu-lation, 57, 62, 63, 109, 110, 114–15, 117; research and development, 8, 115–16; taxes, 71, 73, 96, 121; transfer pricing, 96–97; U.S. corporations, 7–8. *See also* Employment and labor issues; Pharmaceuticals and chemicals indus-tries; Tax issues

Caribbean countries, 69

Caribbean Projects Financing Authority (CARIFA), 84

Census (*1970, 1980, 1990, 2000*; U.S.), 25, 55